Womunafu's Bunafu

WOMUNAFU'S BUNAFU

A Study of Authority in a
Nineteenth-Century African Community

DAVID WILLIAM COHEN

PRINCETON UNIVERSITY PRESS
Princeton, New Jersey

Published by Princeton University Press, Princeton, New Jersey
In the United Kingdom: Princeton University Press,
Guildford, Surrey

Library of Congress Cataloging in Publication Data will
be found on the last printed page of this book

Publication of this book has been aided by a grant from the
Paul Mellon fund of Princeton University Press

This book has been composed in VIP Times Roman

Printed in the United States of America
by Princeton University Press, Princeton, New Jersey

For Susan, Jennifer, and Benjamin

Contents

Maps

Figures and Tables

FIGURES

TABLES

Orthography

Except where common local usage varies, the spelling of proper names follows the modern Lusoga orthography set forward by Gideon I. Byandala, *The Lusoga Orthography* (Iganga, Uganda, 1963), which itself follows standard phonetic rules. In Lusoga and Luganda, stress is usually placed on the first syllable of the stem of the word; that is, on the first syllable after the prefix (*mu-*, *ba-*, *bu-*, *ka-*, *ki-*, *bi-*, *lu-*, *n-*, *m-*, etc.). In Lusoga, "*ky-*" is pronounced as "ch-" in "church."

In conformity with common English practice, prefixes are omitted from Bantu adjectival forms—"Soga," "Nyoro," and "Ganda," instead of "kisoga," "kinyoro," and "kiganda," meaning "of a kind associated with Busoga" (or Bunyoro or Buganda).

For the sake of simplicity, the pre-prefixes *o-*, *e-*, and *a-* have been dropped from most Lusoga and Luganda words used in the text, except where pronunciation is encumbered.

Womunafu's Bunafu

Introduction

THIS volume springs from a brief announcement of marriage. This announcement was not read in the Sunday paper. It did not arrive in elegant dress by post nor is it preserved today in a hall of records. It is the report of a marriage of some 140 years antiquity preserved in the memories of men and women. It is a report communicated by spoken word. This record of the union of Wagubona and his bride Lubagu survives to the present day because various people over several generations felt it sufficiently important to speak of it and because those who listened happened to remember something of what they heard about these two people.

On November 17, 1966, the simple chronicle of this union took another form—recorded on tape by the present writer, a historian interested in recovering the precolonial past of what in this century has been called Busoga District, Uganda. In its transcribed and translated form, the record reads, "Wagubona wanted a woman so he went to Bunafu to a man named Nafa and married a woman named Lubagu."[1] Lubagu, it was later learned, was the daughter of this man Nafa. Nafa himself lived, died, and was buried in the small community called Bunafu. Bunafu is located within the present county and former kingdom of Luuka in west-central Busoga.

The kingdom of Luuka was one of the many centralized states that gave structure and form to the populations of the wider region stretching from the foothills of Mount Elgon on the present Kenya-Uganda border westward around the northern and western shores of Lake Victoria, across what is today Rwanda, and into the eastern regions of the Republic of Zaire (see map 1). The presence of centralized politi-

3

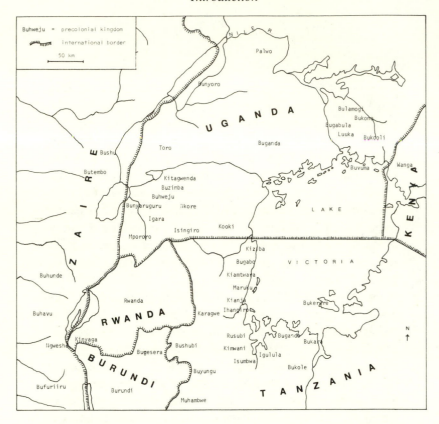

MAP 1 ● The Lake Victoria Region. The region draws its special identity from the strong degree of political centralization achieved in the area before the colonial period. More than a hundred precolonial kingdoms have been identified, some of them with beginnings in the thirteenth and fourteenth centuries. Many of the precolonial states disappeared well before the colonial period, absorbed by stronger polities, and some emerged only in the nineteenth century. The colonial authorities institutionalized the notional boundaries of the precolonial kingdoms, and the various states in the region were introduced into colonial administration as counties, districts, provinces, or protectorates. Some of the precolonial states of the region were so small they cannot be shown on the map.

4

cal institutions in the precolonial era sets this region off from adjoining areas of eastern and central Africa.

Wagubona, the groom, and his father had left their home on the eastern side of the kingdom of Buganda in the early nineteenth century. At that time, Buganda was the most powerful and perhaps the most expansive kingdom in the wider Interlacustrine region, its land area encompassing some 10,000 square kilometers. Luuka was but one of Buganda's close neighbors to the east. (See map 2.) In contrast to Buganda, Luuka was one of the smaller states of the wider region. The Luuka king controlled not more than 400 square kilometers at the time of Wagubona's arrival from Buganda.

There was nothing exceptional about these two Baganda abandoning their home on the eastern side of Buganda, traveling eastward into less familiar worlds across the Nile River. For more than two centuries, Baganda had been fleeing the political troubles within their kingdom—and many fled eastward into what is today Busoga. Likewise, there was nothing particularly startling about Wagubona turning up in the area of Bunafu in what is today Luuka County. The reconstructable migrations in the area of Busoga are myriad—the base of historical tradition for at least half a millennium. The history of this region is, in one sense, the aggregated histories of individuals and groups on the move. These movements cannot be reduced to a simple pattern. But though the reconstruction is inchoate, certain forms, periods, and factors are beginning to be revealed.[2] These were not, as one very distant observer of Africa's past has noted, "unrewarding gyrations,"[3] but rather calculated adventures to acquire land, honor, and status in new places—and, not infrequently, to seek refuge from the tangles of disastrous political maneuvers in a former home.

It is because of this plethora of small-scale migrations that one finds today that the lineages and clans with which

5

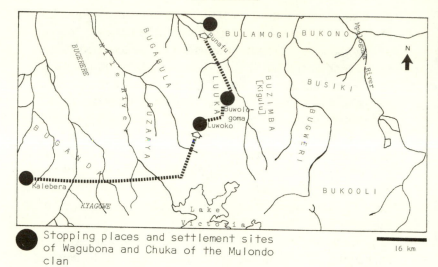

● Stopping places and settlement sites
of Wagubona and Chuka of the Mulondo
clan

■■■■■ Approximate routes taken by Wagubona
and Chuka

B U G W E R I   state

KYAGGWE   district or *ssaza*
                     of·Buganda (today, county)

MAP 2 ● Eastern Buganda and the Busoga States. In the 1890s, on the eve of the colonial era, there were more than sixty states in the region that came to be known as "Busoga." The smallest states were in the south, and most of these were brought within the administration of a single county in the early colonial years. The larger states were in the north and in the east—Bugabula, Luuka, Bulamogi, and Bukooli. Buzaaya had virtually ceased to exist because of depopulation before the 1890s. Busiki, Bugweri, and Buzimba (Kigulu) had been so overwhelmed by civil war in the nineteenth century that they were essentially agglomerations of principalities. In the early colonial period they were reunified. Bukono, a small kingdom in the northeast, was the only state to resist violently the growth of British influence in the 1890s. The map also shows the two most eastern districts of the Buganda kingdom: Bugerere and Kyaggwe. In the early nineteenth century, this region just to the west of the Nile River was not yet fully integrated into the Buganda state. It was from Kalebera in Kyaggwe that Wagubona traveled to Luuka and then to Bunafu.

6

people identify are widely dispersed. Kin residing close to
one another represent little more of the wider group than a
shallow patrilineage. The story of Wagubona's travels indicates that he himself lived for a short time in the south-
ernmost area of the Luuka kingdom before moving to
Bunafu, a site that lay some thirty kilometers to the north,
on the frontier of expansion of the Luuka state in the
nineteenth century. Many of Wagubona's close kin remained behind in Buganda, while some established themselves in the small Soga kingdoms to the east and to the
west of Luuka. In consequence of the dispersed nature of
Soga clans and lineages and of the close political boundaries, the scattered kin of Wagubona (like all dispersed
families in nineteenth-century Busoga) were effectively
without larger, more inclusive corporate structures of kinship.[4]

Wagubona and Lubagu had three sons—born at Bunafu.
It was probably in the 1850s that Wagubona and his sons
and affines moved from the Bunafu area to neighboring
Bugabula, a kingdom lying just to the west of Luuka.
There, Wagubona's three sons achieved some distinction,
eventually being granted control of several village and subvillage chiefships, which their descendants control today.[5]
In Busoga generally, the control of land, villages, and subvillages has been the corporate responsibility of the patrilineage that has emerged around the "man who took control of the land." The control of land and village offices,
which at first was often assigned to individuals by leaders of
the community or officials of the state, has come to be defined within the meaning of lineage inheritance. The owner
of land and office is perceived as a representative of his
lineage, though in fact he may be a founder of a new lineage. Most typically, a son or brother is granted "owner-
ship" upon the previous "owner's" death, though again as
representative of the lineage. The offices granted to the sons

of Wagubona were but three of the more than 1,500 lower-level administrative posts (in certain respects, estates) in the mid-nineteenth-century kingdom of Bugabula. While they were not high offices or positions of great significance within the state of Bugabula, the grants were of sufficient importance to create a tradition of honor within the lineage of Wagubona and to assure the preservation of a record of achievement, including a record of Wagubona's marriage at Bunafu, over some 140 years.

What was striking about this record of the marriage of Wagubona and Lubagu? Beyond its tale of the rise of an estateless refugee from Buganda to a rather honored position in another place, the record was specifically and completely corroborated in traditions preserved by persons and lineages of considerable social distance from the lineage of Wagubona. In Busoga there are not today, and were not in the past, officials charged with the responsibility for recording events, the preservation of these records, or the transmission of such records of the past to future generations. There was, moreover, no written documentation until the 1890s. To some extent everyone was involved in the preservation and transmission of historical information, though not necessarily consciously. The preservation and transmission of such information was not consistent but rather varied according to the relationship of individual or group to particular facets of the past, to the positions of observers and listeners in the past. The preservation of information varied too with the substance and meaning of things past. The capture of a leopard, or at least the specific elements of a hunt tradition, might be quickly forgotten, the rewards spread thin or fleeting (in a sense, nondurable). On the other hand the allocation of a political office and land to a particular person or lineage and the possibly related dispossession of another, were not likely to be forgotten by any of the principal participants in the affair, nor by their descendants. Their

8

place in society and their rights to the office and land were preserved, and are preserved today, not in deeds, papers, or documentary titles of appointment, but in the corroborated memories of men and women around them.

Such information was not, and is not, contained within fixed or highly stylized traditions. Tradition in Busoga is much less the arcane survivals of an oral past than the lively and ever-functioning intelligence upon which society and man rest. The transmission of historical information is not along orderly chains of transmission but across and through the complex networks of relationship, association, and contact that constitute social life.[6]

The testimonies recorded in Busoga relating to the precolonial past, and upon which this volume is mostly based, reflect this character of tradition. These testimonies tend to be loose and weakly structured narratives, collecting together aggregations of data on a variety of topics. Everyone to some extent preserves, and may offer, some material relevant to the reconstruction of the past: a lineage drumbeat slogan; a shrine, place, or personal name; or a record of a marriage or migration. Tradition presents itself to the historian in myriad small pieces and with little in the way of frameworks for synthesis. The absence of specialist informants and highly structured tradition (whether fixed in form or content) does provide, paradoxically, an advantage to the historian. Traditions—or better, what an individual says about the past—tend to be parochial, bound to particular local experience, preserved by residents of a neighborhood and members of a lineage. The continuing dispersal of lineage members makes possible the corroboration of much of the data contained in such a parochial testimony, for assertions may be checked against testimony offered by distant members of dispersed lineages whose ancestors may have shared the experience of the antecedents of the first interviewee.

9

Introduction

Modes of verification are important. While over the past ten or fifteen years it has become widely acknowledged that oral tradition may be usable as a record of the past, the increasing trust placed in such tradition is not based on the presumption that it is equivalent to a literary record, nor is the trust founded upon some recognition of the pristine virtue of the spoken word. Rather, the growing use of oral material in the writing of African history is increasingly based upon an enhanced sophistication in the recording, testing, and analysis of oral testimonies. Historians are giving greater attention to the social role and personality of the informant or interviewee, to the character and structure of the interview or recording session, to the shape, substance, and idiom of oral tradition within the particular culture, and to the possibilities for cross-checking material within oral testimonies with evidence adduced either from other bodies of data or from testimonies that are substantially independent of the testimonies under evaluation.

It was this latter consideration, rather than the inherent persuasiveness of a single, clear, and explicit testimony, that gave weight to, and enlarged the interest in, the record of the marriage of Wagubona and Lubagu. It was an elder of the Muganza clan, the clan of Lubagu the bride, who mentioned in a long narrative recorded some weeks after the first recording of the marriage story that a "man named Nafa once living in a place called Bunafu in Luuka had a daughter named Lubagu. This daughter married a man named Wagubona and they had three sons and left Bunafu and went to Bugabula."[7] Within just a few weeks, then, two people—one of the clan of Wagubona and one of the clan of Lubagu—living some fifteen miles from one another had spoken of this union. That this nineteenth-century man and woman were not great notables, yet that their marriage was so simply and precisely corroborated in tradition, led me, upon returning to Busoga to undertake a second year of re-

10

search beginning in July 1971, to take a fuller look at this link between two families in the village of Bunafu.

The first interviews undertaken in and near Bunafu in this second period of research provided some new data on Wagubona and Lubagu, but more interestingly unveiled a new story. It was a story of a long period of conflict and competition between Nafa (Lubagu's father) and his descendants on the one side and a figure called Womunafu, in fact a prince of the royal house of Luuka, on the other. The struggle focused upon the control of Bunafu, the very place where the marriage union between Wagubona and Lubagu was said to have been consummated. The initial testimonies suggested that by 1870 Womunafu had grasped control of the Bunafu area. In the process, the influence of the family of Nafa was crushed. There was in fact nothing exceptional about this case of a prince wresting authority over a community from earlier "proprietors" such as Nafa's lineage. This was a rather common process in the expansion of royal influence throughout the Lake Victoria region, and in Busoga the histories of many communities were expressed in the gaunt terms of "Prince so-and-so came to this place and took it from someone ruling it at the time." Here Bunafu presented itself as a place where such expansion of royal prerogative, in fact authority, in the precolonial era might be studied in detail.

In those first few days of work in Bunafu in 1971, an intensive study of the Bunafu community in the nineteenth century (incorporating an examination of the career of Womunafu) seemed to promise value beyond the elaboration of evidence on the union of Wagubona and Lubagu, even beyond the paradigmatic struggle between Nafa and Womunafu for control of Bunafu. Bunafu was, in the mid-nineteenth century, on the northern margins of the Luuka kingdom. What was the nature of relations with the Luuka state in the era of Nafa's dominance over the community?

11

What role did the court of Luuka play in the expansion of the kingdom to the north and into the Bunafu area? What networks and institutions functioned in this increasingly significant interplay of political center and northern frontier? These were a few of the core of questions which were written, in much cruder terms, in the corners of notebooks and on scraps of paper during the first days of research in Bunafu. They were not questions one would pose to an interviewee, but they were questions that deepened my interest in Bunafu.

These questions joined what was seen in the first moment as an intensive village study to a wider realm of action and meaning in precolonial Busoga life. Bunafu cannot be taken as a representative community nor as a microcosm of Busoga, Luuka, or African society. Its exceptionality drew attention to its nineteenth-century experience, which broke down my hesitancy to undertake a large interviewing project within a very small area. The nature of the struggles that occurred there suggested that a close study of Bunafu might unveil sections of the historical, social, and particularly, political fabric that interwove court and community, family and society, in the wider region.

Yet Prince Womunafu attracted deeper attention. Womunafu was born with white markings on his arms, the traditions record. According to some sources, he spoke in the womb and was born with teeth. In Busoga the detection of such characteristics of exceptionality bring upon one a recognition of *possession*. In respect to male members of the royal families of northern Busoga, it is called "having the gift of Mukama." This Mukama possession accords one a status embracing a complex of historical, political, and ritual qualities, which in aggregate seem to parallel those qualities of the great folk hero of Busoga popular tradition: Mukama. This heroic Mukama is recalled today in popular tradition as having traveled across the center of Busoga from east to west, attracting along the way an entourage of interested and loyal followers, including clients, wives, in-laws, and servants. In these popular traditions, Mukama is said to have moved west across the Nile River, leaving behind in Busoga a number of sons who are recalled today in popular traditions as the founders of many of the kingdoms of northern Busoga, including Luuka.[8]

Mukama is also the title of the former kings of Bunyoro–Kitara, an area to the west and northwest of Buganda and recalled today as having encompassed a vast part of western Uganda. Finally, the term is a designation of elevated rank, status, and authority across much of Bantu-speaking Africa. The presence of a Mukama figure within the nineteenth-century experience of the Bunafu community offered a small, yet accessible, mirror potentially reflecting outward the character and meaning of the more arcane experience of the earlier Mukama figure and projecting light upon *authority* and *dominance* in one part of a much wider region.

The volume has another axis quite apart from the study of a community and quite apart from the study of patterns of authority. Throughout the period of research and writing from which this volume has emerged, there has persisted a concern, a worry, for the modes of presentation of *past*. It is a concern that comes to the surface only occasionally in the body of the book, yet it is a concern that has affected, even formed, the texture and structure of the volume. What had assumed a central place in an earlier published study of Busoga and again in this study of Bunafu was the remarkable cleft that appeared between the "interior accounts"— Bunafu's presentations of its past—and that rendering of past that was emerging from the historian's reconstruction. What was observed was a distinction between one history of a past and another. What was unobserved, yet sensed, were the workings of individuals, groups, and institutions that affected, shaped, and reformed the shared history of a past, and yet significantly these forces left extant bodies of information from which other, quite different, "pasts" could be rendered. Here, a sharp methodological distinction is made between "history" as a narrative of the past and "past" as that which the historian attempts to reconstruct, comprehend, and represent.

The particular history of Bunafu presented here is not, almost certainly, the history that any person brought up in Bunafu—or the people of Bunafu working collectively— would write. It would be pretentious to imagine, disingenuous to imply, that this volume is an enlarged interior account. Much of the information that Bunafu's past has left for the historian falls outside that knowledge of past that informs Bunafu's own presentations of history. The information the past has left for us, which is used in this reconstruction, includes data on the environment, the locations of settlements, migrations, marriages, developments away from Bunafu, and the meanings of words and phenomena. This is not to say that the people of Bunafu are unaware of their environment, that they are ignorant of the locations of their compounds, or that they are without knowledge of where their antecedents may have lived before traveling to Bunafu. This is in fact crucial information in this society, and it is in part because of its significance that considerable information from the past is present for the historian to collect and use. The point is that such familiar, such parochial, information does not lie within the mental compartments from and through which the past is perceived, understood, and presented in the form of conscious history by the people of Bunafu.

There is another reason why this reconstruction of Bunafu's past is different from Bunafu's own rendering of past. In a very important sense, historical presentation constitutes a simplification of the complex nature of past, though our students sometimes believe it to be the other way around. The point is simply that different people carry in their heads different modes and systems of arranging and simplifying the complex and massive information that the past remits to the living. In contradistinction to Bunafu's rendering of past, this present reconstruction follows a formal chronological axis and is selective of elements of the past that inform the study of *authority*.

There are also differences between the structure of this volume as a history and the fairly well established models of presentation of African communities and societies in the social sciences, particularly in the disciplines of history and anthropology. In respect to Africa as a field of study, these two disciplines have remarkably different life histories. A first and simple observation is that anthropology, in the dress of ethnography and social anthropology, came of age in Africa long before the discipline of history. More significantly, the field of anthropology in Africa developed within a Eurocentric milieu in which other people's pasts were not considered significant, in an epistemological milieu in which it was felt that other cultures could be understood without detailed reference to the past, and in a colonial milieu in which it was felt that change could be controlled. Synchronic "models" of African societies were thus multiply reinforced, and the anthropological monograph came to conform to a synchronist model of presentation. The past or history was noted as a sort of preface to "society" or to "structure," while the intense force of the past upon the present was ignored. Change was viewed in terms of policy formation rather than as part of structure, and the more simple relationships between elements of the past remarked upon in the historical preface and elements of the present discussed in the body of the monograph were typically passed over lightly.

As noted, the historical study of African societies came

rather late. Far from being handicapped, historians have in fact had the advantage of a deep and informed literature on Africa produced by earlier research in anthropology. But what has happened too often—and the present writer includes himself here—is that in the more recent historical writing on African societies, the anthropologist's synchronic model has been transcended only in so far as it has been stood on its head. Historians have misperceived social structure and culture as the *contexts* within which event, change, and development occurred. In terms of literary presentation of the past, this perceived context is often described in the form of a preface or an introduction to the historian's monograph. Such an identification and utilization of context can be quite conscious, for in respect to the study of the African past the historian's craft is constrained by the very weight and importance of the existing anthropological literature, by the obligation to inform the reader of the very different world of the African society that is in view, and by the burden of making explicit those innumerable "understoods," which are simply givens in the deep and literate historiographical traditions of other fields of history. This meretricious *separation* of culture, context, and structure from change and development therefore remains a persistent force and flaw in the presentation of Africa in the literature of the social sciences, even as the historical discipline supplants anthropology at the formative center of that literature.

The problem for the historian is, however, something more than supplanting synchrony with diachrony or extending a time dimension from a relatively well known baseline. The problem is that it is easy and erroneous to take the descriptions and analyses of life and institutions contained within the monographs of a generation of social anthropologists as objective reality. It is less easy now, for modern ethnographers have been more cautious than their

16

disciplinary forebears in making explicit the representational or "modeling" aspects of their enterprise. Their intent is not to reproduce reality but rather to place within a system of comprehension that reality that is perceived. For some, that system of comprehension is drawn from an exogenous notion of what is important and what categories of information, analysis, and presentation will join the field study to wider questions. This intent affects and shapes all of anthropological work, whether or not the authors have made explicit such intent. Given this, the historian would err in taking as context those anthropological descriptions and analyses that are essentially abstractions from, or simplifications of, reality.

This two-headed gift of anthropology to the discipline of history cannot, however, be set aside as one tries to recover and understand "what really happened." The existing anthropological literature—what is said, what is written, what is known, what is understood—does affect, does inform, our very approaches and assumptions. These approaches and assumptions have the power to sort the important from the less important, the central from the extraneous, reality from unreality. What is attempted in this volume is a return to the evidence bearing on what happened so as to allow that evidence to contribute to a rendering of the "moving contexts" of the past and to allow those reconstructed moving contexts to inform a discussion of authority. This methodology is carried over into the form of presentation. The reader will find neither the historical preface of the anthropological monograph nor the ethnographic preface of the historical study. Rather, an attempt is made to present context and change as both moving and one—to tell and inform within one structure of presentation.

The decision to go beyond the first few interviews in Bunafu and to embark upon a more precisely defined study of the community in the nineteenth century conflicted to some extent with research commitments in other parts of Busoga. This permitted only intermittent work in Bunafu, approximately six weeks in aggregate over the eight months between July 1971 and March 1972. The interviewing programs elsewhere in Busoga did, however, permit adjustment of the schedule to include the tracking down of additional information on particular immigrant and emigrant families associated in one way or another with Bunafu. This interviewing served both to enlarge the base of data available to the Bunafu study and to provide material for the testing of data collected in Bunafu. In addition, extensive and able assistance was provided by a research assistant based in Bunafu between September and November 1971.

The study, then, is based upon material collected in several hundred interviews undertaken in Bunafu and neighboring communities during 1971-72, upon some 200 interviews undertaken outside the Bunafu area but still within Luuka in 1966-67 and 1971-72, and upon a large number of interviews undertaken outside Luuka County but within the District of Busoga during the two research periods. Less tangibly, months of observation along with rambling conversation and itinerant listening and incessant questioning in less formal settings could not but have affected the shape and content of this study.

This book is dedicated to the vitality of Bunafu's past and to the people of Bunafu who once lived and now live, whose experiences will for a long time shape the lives of people living within Bunafu. Grateful acknowledgment is made to the men, women, and children who offered intimate and sensitive and important material to the historian and in so doing showed faith and trust that an outsider would somehow pull together the thousands of loose ends and "get the story right." In doing so, the people of Bunafu revealed the value they themselves place in this exercise in making sense of, and drawing meaning from, the past. Unconsciously, in certain respects consciously, they generated a fusion between a past that is alive and a past that may also be studied, ultimately perhaps considered, reconsidered, and understood. In generating this fusion, they placed considerable responsibility in the hands of the historian, a responsibility that I recognize is unequivocally mine.

Gratitude must also be expressed to the John Simon Guggenheim Memorial Foundation and to the Department of History and the Institute of Southern History of the Johns Hopkins University, which together made possible a second year of research in Busoga and thus this intensive study of Bunafu. The Central Research Fund of the University of London and the School of Oriental and African Studies of that university generously supported the 1966-67 research. Recognition and appreciation are due my assistants in the field during 1971-72: Abud-Magidu Nkaaye, Alex Mutalya, and Bosis Galyaki. Warm thanks are also due Chris and Julie Jeffrey and E. Basil Boothby who made available in their homes quiet retreats during times when diverse obligations made traditional habitats unsuited to writing.

In less material ways, my colleagues in the Department of History and the Department of Anthropology at the Johns Hopkins University—faculty and students—not only gave me considerable encouragement but also, over the past few years, opened to me realms of learning and perspective that have helped me better understand, and made me better able to seek to understand, meaning in the past. Rhys Isaac, Edward C. Carter, Orest Ranum, Jan Vansina, Roland Oliver, Richard Price, David Kiyaga-Mulindwa, Richard Sigwalt, Elinor Sosne, Lou Rojas, Gene Galbraith, and Ira Lowenthal read the manuscript and made helpful suggestions, for which of course I am grateful. In material, yet also more than material ways, Susan Hadary Cohen contributed enor-

19

mously to the completion of this book, rearranging her own time and work so that a household might survive, and contributing spirit and energy to the enterprise of writing this volume, even when it meant less time for her own writing.

David William Cohen
Baltimore, Maryland
August 1976

I

The Birth of Womunafu

AT the close of the eighteenth century, Luuka was a small
and weak state. Political control was felt over distances
no greater than thirty kilometers. To the west, south, and
east, swamp-filled valleys constituted major obstacles to
expansion. (See map 3.) To the north, the Nabisira River
marked the frontier of regular administration. The Nabisira
is a funnel which carries away excess water from the adjacent lands to the north and south. In the drier months the
Nabisira resembles a long narrow swamp. In the two wet
seasons of the year, the Nabisira becomes a papyrus-
rimmed stream, carrying water away toward the east and
depositing it in the northward-flowing Lumbuye River. The
great Lumbuye, which separates western and central
Busoga today, was always a substantial obstacle to movement east and west. The Nabisira, in comparison, presented
no great inconvenience to those who sought to cross it. At
Busanda on the east, there was a ford which was firm and
easy during the two dry seasons of the year; at Makutu in
the center there was a year-round shallow water track; and
at Nawanhago along the western reaches of the river, it was
possible to make a dry crossing most times of the year. (See
map 4.) The river itself was no barrier to the expansion of
the Luuka state, but its location some thirty kilometers north
of the capitals of the Luuka kings made it the northern limit
of expansion of the state in this period.

The Nabisira was also a horizon. While the early kings of
Luuka clearly could not administer the region beyond the
Nabisira, by the close of the eighteenth century their atten-
tions were occasionally oriented in this direction. The sec-

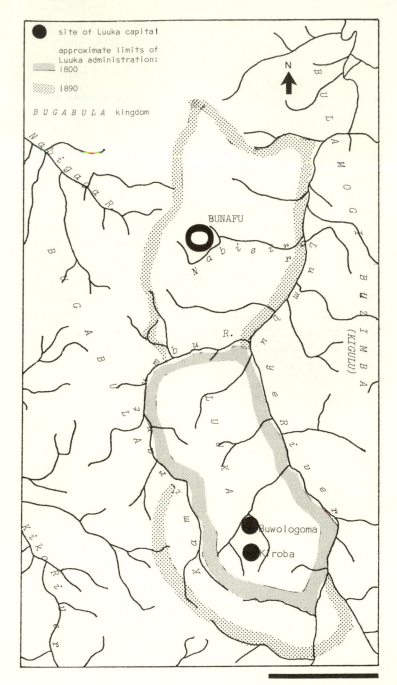

site of Luuka capital

approximate limits of
Luuka administration:
1800

1890

BUGABULA kingdom

N

BUNAFU

BUGABULA

Nabigaga R.

Nabisira R.

Mbuzi R.

LUUKA

Nsenge River

BULAMOGI

*BUZIMBA
(KIGULU)*

Buwologoma

Kiroba

Kikori R.

Kuma River

10 km

MAP 3 ● The Luuka Kingdom in the Nineteenth Century. The Luuka kingdom more than doubled in size in the period between 1800 and 1890. At the beginning of the nineteenth century, the Luuka kingdom had yet to expand beyond the major rivers that formed its boundaries, though interest was already being shown in the lands north of the Kamirantumbu and Nabisira rivers. The administration of Luuka never extended eastward beyond the great Lumbuye River. Westward expansion was limited by the competitive interests of Luuka's neighbor, Bugabula. The map shows the approximate limits of expansion of the Luuka kingdom in about 1800 and again about 1890. The locations of the capitals of the first three rulers of Luuka are also noted. Kiroba, the first capital, was occupied by all three rulers—Nhiro, Inhensiko I, and Wambuzi. Inhensiko I also occupied a second capital which he built at Buwologoma.

ond ruler of Luuka had sent his dedicated follower Kalalu north of the Nabisira as a first effort to bring the area to the north under the control of the Luuka capital. Kalalu was a commoner, a man of the Muluuta clan, one of a few migrants from the Lake Victoria coastlands to reach so far north before 1800. He established a home at Nasumiti, now called Budhuuba, at the northern edge of the Nabisira swamp.[1] Over the next three generations the Muluuta chiefs at Nasumiti would bring most of the northern reaches of the region under the administrative control of the Luuka kings.

The second ruler of Luuka—Inhensiko—accelerated the program of expansion to the north through a strategic marriage. Kabalu was a young girl—of the Munhana clan. Her family had fled Bugweri in the center of Busoga some two generations before her birth.[2] They settled at Nsambya on the Nakaibaale, a stream flowing southward into the Nabisira. Living to the north of the Nabisira, Kabalu's family was beyond the control of Inhensiko and, before him, his father Nhiro. Nevertheless, they sought contact with the Luuka capital—the gift of Kabalu to King Inhensiko was an early invitation to the ruler to formalize his influence north of the

23

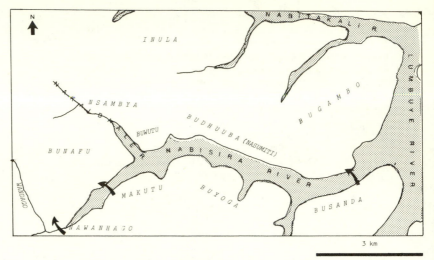

I N U L A   mutala (section of raised land, village)

fords across the
Nabisira

Map 4 ● The Nabisira Valley. In the early nineteenth century, the Nabisira River valley lay beyond the regular administration of the Luuka state. Only at Budhuuba was a representative of the Luuka kings on the scene, though the mother of King Wambuzi did come from Nsambya. The Nabisira flowed eastward into the Lumbuye, which is one of the great rivers of Busoga carrying water north into Lake Kyoga. The tributaries and rivers of Busoga are in fact papyrus-filled valleys with narrow water courses. During the wet seasons the narrow water courses broaden and deepen, and during the dry seasons they become quite shallow, permitting fording at a number of points. The dry-season fords are located on the map. The fords at Nawanhago and Makutu were passable in most wet periods as well. The Lumbuye River could not be forded except in the driest of years.

Nabisira. Kabalu traveled to Inhensiko's enclosure at Kiroba Hill, and there she became the senior, though not the first, wife in the palace upon his accession to kingship. Her son Wambuzi Munhana (as he was eventually called) was

24

one of the many sons born to Inhensiko and his many wives during his long reign. Sixteen sons survived to maturity, but as the eldest surviving son of the senior wife, Wambuzi was in the best position to succeed to the throne upon his father's death. He spent much of his childhood north of the Nabisira in his mother's home at Nsambya. His presence there not only protected him from the dangers of palace strife and foreign wars, but also served to extend the influence of the ruling house of Luuka into the Nsambya area.

Inhensiko's reign was a long and active one, and Wambuzi was well along in years when his father finally passed away within his home at Kiroba Hill. Wambuzi was probably taken at night across thirty kilometers of countryside between Nsambya and Kiroba by his mother Kabalu, his Munhana brothers-in-law, the Muluuta chief at Nasumiti (then still, apparently, Kalalu), and a collection of other supporters.[3] A long reign had given King Inhensiko and his followers various opportunities to prepare the way for Wambuzi's succession. The other sons were increasingly isolated from contact with the palace as Inhensiko advanced in years. They may not have been informed of their father's death until it was too late. Wambuzi most likely reached the palace on the day following his father's passing. He was soon thereafter seated on Inhensiko's throne at Kiroba Hill without resistance.

It was about the fifteenth year of Wambuzi's reign— some time in the third decade of the nineteenth century— when a small house was erected on the edge of the Nabisira swamp on the northern margins of the Luuka state. The house was constructed quickly of reeds and grass cut from the margins of the swamp, and it was sited in a small clearing near the Makutu crossing of the Nabisira. This was a rough shelter, the kind that new settlers in Busoga put up for themselves until they can put together the materials, time, and assistance to erect a larger and more lasting building.

This particular shelter was built for a young woman named Mukanni. Mukanni was a commoner—of the Igobe clan—and her family's home and the home of her birth lay just across the Nabisira from Makutu.[4] She was being taken home to her father and to her brothers, but she was undoubtedly anxious, worried, confused, seeking the safety and warmth of her home, yet concerned about arriving there pregnant. Mukanni had disgraced herself at home some years before. There may have been an earlier illicit pregnancy. Exiled from her home, too young and ill informed to seek out the protection of relatives elsewhere, she eventually reached the palace of Wambuzi. She joined the palace staff as maid and whore. There, tradition records, her small figure and enormous breasts attracted the attentions of most of the men in the palace, including Wambuzi. Wambuzi was particularly interested in her lovely body, tradition tells us, and he slept with her on a number of occasions. Within a year of her arrival in the palace, Wambuzi noticed that Mukanni was pregnant. For some reason he felt embarrassed, even threatened by the situation, and he ordered his closest advisors to remove her from the palace and "dispose of her."[5] The assignment was an ambiguous one—the words of instruction could mean many things: should she be sold off, should she be returned to her home, should she be killed? For the advisors the problem was a difficult one; Mukanni was carrying a member of the royal family. The traditions suggest, moreover, that Wambuzi wanted to hear nothing about the decision finally made. It was a closed subject, or at least so it appeared.

We cannot explore the minds of the advisors of Wambuzi, and we cannot know with precision the reasons why Mukanni was not sold off or killed. We do know she was not harmed. There certainly were people at the court—people of influence—who did not want to see Mukanni "disposed of," who did not want to see her and her child extinguished, who saw opportunity in the birth of yet another prince, even an illegitimate one. Wambuzi had six sons already, and several of these were, by the time of Mukanni's pregnancy, vying for their father's title. It may be assumed that each son was a rallying point for intrigue at the palace, for adventurers arriving in Luuka sought to enhance their status through forming alliances with, and aiding the rise of, potential successors. Some may have sought to attach themselves to a prince who could possibly ensure them land, status, and office in the region north of the Nabisira where Mukanni's kin were established. This particular unborn child would have served the immediate needs of these adventurers, for it was recognized that it was a male, a prince, and that he had "spoken in the womb"; not only spoken, but that he had, in fact, requested regalia, the symbols of royal office. The hearing of the words from the womb and the recognition of possession wove a protective shroud around the pregnant Mukanni, at the same time narrowing the choices available to Wambuzi's advisors. They would not kill Mukanni. The unborn child would be protected.

It was evidently determined that the unborn prince would be best protected at his mother's home just north of the Makutu crossing of the Nabisira. There was nothing novel in this decision to return Mukanni, with the unborn prince, to her home. This was the ideal for the royal families of the states located right across northern Busoga—that a son of a ruler should be raised at his mother's home. Born in the palace, yes; raised in the palace, no. Ibanda Ngobi, the father of the founders of the ruling houses of the Luuka and Kigulu kingdoms was raised at Nhenda Hill in the fenced compound of the father of Tegula, the girl who was his mother. Inhensiko I, the second ruler of Luuka, was raised at his mother's home, and his sixteen sons were brought up in the compounds of their mothers. Wambuzi Munhana, Inhensiko I's successor, was raised at Nsambya, at the home of his mother, Kabalu.

The raising of these princes at the homes of their mothers served to bridge the prestigious bearing and exogenous culture of the northern ruling families in Busoga with the commoner homes of the Bantu-speaking local families. In the reigns of the first rulers of Luuka (and of the first rulers of the other kingdoms of northern Busoga), two worlds coexisted. The first was the world of the enclosure where the values, the ideas, the cultural fabric of Lwo-speaking people were sustained. These Lwo speakers and their non-Lwo-speaking children were the descendants of migrants who had dispersed far and wide from the southern Sudan and northern Uganda over the preceding eight centuries and whose influence is noted today as far north as Khartoum and as far south as northern Tanzania.[6]

The second world was that of the commoner families, whose Bantu speech and more settled lives gave them a distinct orientation. But these distinctions between coresident Lwo and Bantu could not survive. Royal men married local women and, as fathers, the princes and rulers played little part in the raising of their children. The sons of Mukama, the sons of Ibanda Ngobi, the sons of Inhensiko, and the sons of Wambuzi were born in one world and raised in the other. In the course of two or three or four generations, the Lwo world became increasingly less sustainable, and the royal enclosure lost its cultural distinctiveness. The raising of sons outside the palace bridged rulers and commoners and constituted one of the paths along which the rulers exchanged prestigious isolation for practiced domination.

At the same time, these bridges spanning the gulf between ruler and commoner served to protect the ruler from the ambitions of his royal brothers. Bearing royal status, the ruler's kin were difficult to discipline and not infrequently sought separate status through secession and civil conflict.[7]

28

The circle of involved and trusted commoners, tied to the ruler through marriage, served to protect him from the ambitions of his royal kin. These commoner in-laws could be used to discipline recalcitrant princes in times of civil war or in disputes over succession. It was Inhensiko I who first and most extensively utilized this principle of alliance. His sweeping network of marriages brought to his side new and trusted followers, many of them—as in the case of Kabalu's family—from outside the existing domain. Inhensiko placed some of these immigrants in important territorial offices, the duties of which included overseeing princes residing within the division. While all of Inhensiko's sons were granted village estates and enjoyed substantial authority within them, commoners such as Kalalu—the Muluuta clan client of Inhensiko—were given chiefly offices outranking those of the sons of the ruler. This striking insertion of commoner clients between the ruler and his royal kin was the great hallmark of the reign of Inhensiko I.

In giving precedence to delegated authority as opposed to inherited status, Inhensiko I tempered the alliance between a prince and his mother's family among whom he was raised. This in turn opened the way to more formal incorporation into the Luuka kingdom of the areas within which Inhensiko's sons were raised. King Inhensiko and his closest followers had created a new style of politics within the emerging kingdom, one joining the traditional ideal of grooming princes away from the palace to a heightened recognition of the potential role for commoners within the state and an increased concern for discipline within the royal family. Within a generation, Inhensiko I had transformed the world from the Luuka Hills to the Nabisira River, had exchanged his father's prestigious, enclosed isolation and Lwo orientation for full involvement in the world outside the enclosure.

In turn, Inhensiko's son, Wambuzi Munhana, maintained

29

this recognition of the crucial importance of the commoner within the kingdom. Trusted commoners had prepared the way for his own peaceful investiture, and commoner officials were continuing the process of expansion of the state begun in his father's reign. But the tasks of commoners within the kingdom were nonetheless complex and delicate. Princes were above commoners in the arena of social status, yet commoners were charged with the responsibility for disciplining princes in the arena of politics. The incongruence between role and office was not neatly resolved. Innovations and traditions that could weave together the very different fabrics of appointed power and exalted and inherited status into a larger and still stable political realm tended to be affirmed by Inhensiko I and Wambuzi Munhana when dealing with their kin and clients. In this sense, it was politic to permit, even encourage, the ruler's wives to raise their sons at their homes away from the palace. There, the prince might gain a local following and enjoy local power, but such authority would be limited by both the competitive activities of other princes and the commanding presence of a commoner overseer loyal to the king. When Wambuzi's trusted advisors decided to lead Mukanni, with unborn child, back to her home north of the Nabisira, it was, then, a response to an ambiguous assignment worked out within a framework of strategic norms.

But if this was their intention, why did the party halt at the southern bank of the Nabisira, less than 3,000 meters from Mukanni's home? Even in a normal rainy season, the river could be crossed, and even if Mukanni were already in labor, the last stage of the journey would take no more than two hours, considerably less time than it would take to clear the ground and construct a sturdy shelter. Perhaps the explanation lies in concerns we may suppose weighed heavily on the minds of Mukanni and her companions. First, the lands on the other side of the river, where the homes of

Mukanni's family were located, may have been unfamiliar political ground to the men of King Wambuzi. Nearby Nsambya, Wambuzi Munhana's home for some years, was presumably well known but not the lands to the west and southwest of Nsambya; that is, to the northwest of Makutu. This was Nafa's place. Nafa was of the Muganza clan, a strong man in the area just to the northwest of Makutu. (See map 5.) He had had, apparently, no links of any kind with the rulers of Luuka, had sent no girls to Inhensiko's or Wambuzi's compounds, presumably paid no tax or tribute to either Wambuzi or Kalalu at nearby Nasumiti.[8] Could Nafa in fact be a representative in this area of Kagoda, the ruler of "Budiope" (Bugabula) which lay to the west and northwest of Luuka, much as Kalalu was the trusted representative of Wambuzi along the northern horizon of Luuka? Whatever the evidence before the men of Wambuzi, Nafa's world was clearly beyond the boundaries of Luuka, and the crossing of a party from the palace into Nafa's world could only be construed as a serious intrusion.

Moreover, it could not be expected that Mukanni's father, living in the midst of Nafa's world and having himself previously expelled Mukanni, would urge Nafa to welcome the king's party. Mukanni herself probably had serious second thoughts about returning to the abusive atmosphere at home, which a year or two before had driven her away. And her companions may have fretted about the propriety of a prince being born at his mother's home outside the royal domain, something that had not occurred previously. So, very likely the outcome of the play of several concerns rather than merely the exigency of labor, the house was built at Makutu on the southern banks of the river, and there Mukanni had her child.

Even before its birth, tradition tells us, this child of Mukanni had been recognized as "possessed."[9] More significantly, the child was considered to be suffering from, or

31

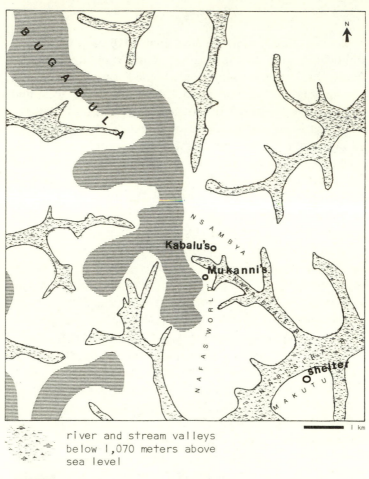

river and stream valleys
below 1,070 meters above
sea level

ridge, at least 1,100
meters above sea level

MAP 5 ● Beyond the Nabisira. At the time of the birth of Mukanni's child at Makutu, the Luuka state had no authority in the region to the northwest of Makutu, beyond the Nabisira. This was Nafa's world. To the north and west of Nafa's domain lay the eastern margins of the Bugabula kingdom, which in this period was expanding east and south down the ridge of higher ground. Mukanni's kin were of the Igobe clan and resided within the area that was Nafa's below the ridge. The site of the compound Mukanni had left when she traveled to Wambuzi's palace is noted on the map. At Nsambya lived the "mothers" of King Wambuzi.

possessed by "Mukama." In Busoga today, the birth of a child possessed by Mukama attracts wide attention. People from far and wide pack beer, food, and gifts and travel to the site of the birth. The gifts are offered to the child and to the deities that play roles in the ritual of birth. Specialists arrive to offer advice and to complete their ritual assignments; some of their work is understood by all in attendance, some is mysterious.

Perhaps most importantly, a substantial number of men contribute a considerable investment of labor and time in the erection of an enclosure for the child possessed by the spirit of Mukama. The enclosure transforms the environment of the child so as to resemble that of the first Mukama, the heroic Lwo figure—tradition recalls—who crossed Busoga from east to west with his large retinue. At a number of sites right across Busoga, large enclosures were built for Mukama. This new Mukama—the illegitimate son of Mukanni and Wambuzi Munhana, the great-great-grandson of the heroic Mukama—was in his turn accorded the exalted isolation of the enclosure while still an infant.

There were many "Bakama" across northern Busoga. Ritual specialists, called *baswezi*, spied out the possessed members of the royal families: cripples, miscreants, those with skin blemishes or teeth at birth or other exceptional indications that could be taken as signs of possession by Mukama. Mukama possessed only males and only members of the royal families of the northern kingdoms.[10]

In some instances, the detection of possession by Mukama was made in adolescence or even adulthood. In most cases, however, it seems that the determination of possession by Mukama was made at birth, or soon thereafter. But in some few cases, the detection of possession was made before the birth, the indication: "speaking in the womb." The case of Mukanni and her unborn child was all the more extraordinary in terms of diagnosis for not only

33

was the detection of possession made before birth—which we might take as a device that protected Mukanni from an early death—but, still more impressively, the original diagnosis was sustained at birth when it was noted that the new-born infant had milk-colored markings on his forearms. Such marking has been the most outstanding sign of possession by the spirit of Mukama.

Thus, the *baswezi* priests who had come to Makutu would have been kept busy, presiding over well-attended ritual.[11] Tradition casts an image of excitement, possibly pandemonium. We learn that the possessed infant, through his *baswezi* intermediaries, ordered his father—King Wambuzi—to visit Makutu and acknowledge his birth. Wambuzi was asked to bring a range of quintessential gifts: a royal barkcloth tree which was to be planted to the right of Mukanni's house to nourish itself on the buried placenta of the new Mukama. A royal spear was ordered, so was a royal shield. The king was instructed to send a three-legged stool, musicians, insignia drums, and a red cow.[12] The priests at Makutu sought—the traditions suggest—to encircle the young prince with the symbols of highest office, to efface instantly the taints of illegitimacy, to alter the stance of the silent and distant Wambuzi. Here we may note further indications of conflict between the enormous and suddenly elaborated prestige of this new Mukama and the authority of the political office of the king of Luuka. Throughout the societies of precolonial Busoga, the idea of Mukama is in curious conflict with the principle of kingship. Mukama is seen as the founder of the states of northern Busoga. But Mukama is also the prestigious figure, the milker, the herdsman, the hunter, the possessed one, the miscreant, the one for whom great enclosures are built, the hero figure who attracts followers and wives, the prolific and generous father, the progenitor of large families, and grantor of estates to his sons here and there. The idea of the possessed

Mukama devolves from the Mukama figure who crossed Busoga, but so does the ascribed status of rulership, encompassing the complex of ideas of prestige over which were fabricated the institutions of state. Tracing descent from the same figure enclosed in prestigious isolation, the new Mukama and the king are none the less substantially different. The king is surrounded by a circle of trusted followers, the possessed Mukama by a covey of *baswezi* who are outside the boundaries of control of the earthly ruler and beyond the control of the ruler's advisors and the ruler's subordinate chiefs. The king's status is received from father or close sibling, the Mukama's status is received through possession and may touch a male member of the royal clan at any kinship distance from ruler, antecedent Mukama, or contemporaneous Mukama. The king's power is focused on a stable center, a capital, while the prestige and authority of a Mukama figure is mobile. The king's authority and status may pass to his sons and close kin. The Mukama's inherent status as a possessed figure does not necessarily pass to his offspring.

In a variety of ways, then, these two historically linked roles tend to be markedly distinguished; and they are potentially opposed. In this instance, it appears that the detection of possession in Mukanni's unborn child was a challenge hurled in the face of Wambuzi. King Wambuzi's tools of power had been honed to deal with foreign enemies and recalcitrant princes but not with the sudden and marvelous appearance of a new node of competitive influence in the form of his own illegitimate son. A direct attack on a possessed Mukama would be an attack on much of his own symbolic garment of prestige.

Conflict between religious and political nodes of authority and influence is, of course, a very widespread phenomenon, the two estates offering eternal and legitimate contexts for the periodic formation of coalitions of opposition to concentrations of authority. Throughout the Lake Victoria world of East Africa, however, these estates are less clearly demarcated—the political and religious realms are both overlapping and in conflict. On the one hand, rulers in pre-colonial Africa are generally considered to have drawn a good measure of legitimacy from divine sources. In the eyes of nineteenth-century European travelers in Africa, the exaggerated bases of political authority—including divine origin, racial distinctions between ruler and conqueror and conquered, practiced domination, and the controls of instruments of life and death—accorded African rulers unbridled power within the boundaries of their domains.[13] But what was not noticed by early European observers such as Stanley and Speke was that the ruler's control of legitimizing symbols, upon which their power and tenure of office rested, was not absolute. The mother of the king—the queen mother—shared his ascription as ruler. Members of his royal family shared his inherited status. Moreover, as symbols of power are most often transferred into comprehensible form through ritual or ceremony, the ritual specialists with training, expertise, and unusual gifts were charged with the critical responsibilities of transforming objects into ideas and maintaining the meaning of symbols. As ritual specialists, they stood at the margins of the apparatus of the state and were no doubt able to view the state in wider contexts. Ritual forms and religious ideas were drawn from the world at large, not from the transient court, not even perhaps from the society described by the state's political boundaries.[14] Ritual, religion, had the potential for coalescing durable and effective opposition to the court at moments of crisis. This may be seen right across the Lake Victoria region and, as we shall see, in the experience of the small Bunafu community.

In Busoga, the new-born infant is not brought out of the house within which it is born until it is some two to eight

weeks old, depending on the timing of the birth in relation
to the millet sowing and harvesting seasons and to the particular practice customary to the family. This delay serves a
practical function, providing a second womb to protect the
infant from the dangers of the world at large during its first
weeks of life. The infant remains, in essence, symbolically
unborn, and if it should die before being brought out of the
house, it is not acknowledged as having ever lived or died.
The coming out of the house, which constitutes the second,
and social, birth, is an important moment. The father must
be present since this ceremony marks the occasion of the
first intercourse of mother and father following the biologi-
cal birth of the child.

For the birth of Mukama, the coming out is still longer
deferred, for the father of the child should not look at his
son the Mukama until he has grown out of infancy, which of
course means a delay of several years. Tradition records
that the Mukama of Mukanni and Wambuzi was not brought
out of the house until he was three years old. He was then
adorned with a necklace of cowrie shells, the insignia of the
baswezi, and was bathed in milk and beer "to prove that he
was a real prince," a man of Lwo culture in the midst of a
non-Lwo world.[15]

We may assume that the coming out of Mukanni's child
presented obvious difficulties to a father who happened also
to be a ruler. Wambuzi had sent Mukanni away from the
palace in ignominy, thereby rejecting her offspring. The infant was beginning life with an exceptional base of influence, which challenged the prestige and authority of the
king himself, and we may assume that Wambuzi was un-
willing to weaken his own stance by openly recognizing the
child. It is, in fact, not clear whether Wambuzi ever hum-
bled himself to visit his illegitimate son Mukama at Makutu
or ever sent along the symbolic offerings demanded. The
traditions only suggest a continuing effort on the part of the

following of the infant Mukama to garner the recognition of the king. There are, nonetheless, various indications that Wambuzi sensed the potential influence of his seventh son and, with his advisors, contrived a plan to make the most of this challenge to his authority: granting the young child an estate northwest of the Nabisira within, or just a few hundred meters to the north of, the small world of Nafa.

II

The World of Nafa

AT the time the shelter was erected at Makutu, Nafa's world constituted a small collection of settlements located on the shallow hillslopes directly across the Nabisira from the birthplace of the new Mukama. Nafa's community was marked off on its eastern flank by the narrow and marshy Nakaibaale, and across the Nakaibaale lay Nsambya, residence of the "mothers" of King Wambuzi of Luuka. To the west and southwest, Nafa's lands were enclosed by the northwestern reaches of the Nabisira.

It is hardly remarkable that narrow bands of stream and swamp should give locational identity to the small community centered on Nafa or that the Nabisira valley should constitute a boundary or horizon of the expanding Luuka state. The coincidence of natural phenomena—streams, swamps, rivers, and lakeshores—with political and administrative frontiers is a characteristic of preindustrial political organization. Across the wider Lake Victoria region of East Africa, swamp and shoreline were the convenient, familiar, and persistent boundary markers of administrative subdivisions within states and the mutually recognized borders between states. Only occasionally does tradition record the maintenance of boundaries surveyed and demarcated by public or private action and preserved through the memories of elderly witnesses to land transactions, adjudications, and conquests.[1] Rather, political structures appear to have rested more typically upon consensual notions of space and control, which accented universally recognizable boundaries such as swamp, river, and shoreline. The significance of natural boundaries like the Nabisira and the Nakaibaale was obviously further enlarged by the limiting effects that even a narrow band of swamp could have upon travel, communication, military expansion, and regular administration—given the potential, even persistent, weakness of political centers throughout the region.

But at certain points, there were no distinctive natural boundaries to mark off frontiers of action, communication, and administration. Examining the locations of interstate conflicts during the second half of the nineteenth century, one notes that skirmishes occurred most frequently in areas that lacked distinctive natural boundaries. These were, essentially, "ambiguous zones," belonging naturally to no state in particular, but ultimately claimed by two or more. The lands above the Nabisira became just such an ambiguous zone. To the north and northwest of Nafa's settlements, there was and is no close, distinctive natural boundary. Rather, the land rises steadily from the valley floor (some 1,067 meters above sea level) to the crests of a long ridge some 1,128 to 1,143 meters above sea level and extending fifteen kilometers to the northwest. (See map 5, chapter I.)

The absence of a close, distinctive, and protective natural boundary on the northwest flank of Nafa's community opened a large area to settlers from the north and west. These settlers carried the imprimatur of the expanding Bugabula state. At first hugging the northwest reaches of the ridge on the margins of Bugabula, they were, at the time of Mukama's birth, expanding southeastward along the crest of the ridge. This expansion, contemporaneous with the construction of a large enclosure for Wambuzi's son, Mukama, opened the ridge to competitive tensions between the expanding Bugabula and Luuka states, tensions that would occasionally be intensified by warfare over the subsequent seventy years. It was within this ambiguous space, on the shallow hillslopes above the Nabisira at the southeastern end of the long ridge, that Nafa's community was located.

40

Perhaps as early as the last years of the eighteenth century, members of the lineage of Nafa and their companions had begun to occupy and control the eastern and southern faces of the ridge. In selecting locations for their shelters, compounds, and gardens, they appear to have hugged the easternmost margins of the ridge and at the same time to have chosen an environment that offered a particularly attractive range of agricultural possibilities. The moist hillslopes tended, in their natural state, to be enclosed by woodland down to the edge of the papyrus-filled valleys. When partially cleared by man, these hillslopes offered an environment well suited to the cultivation of both moist forest food crops and millets. The two rainy seasons—there are two cycles of wet and dry periods in Busoga within the 365-day Julian year—together bring down some 100 centimeters of rain. The rains come occasionally in heavy squalls, unleashing as much as ten centimeters within a few hours. The water rushes down the hillslopes, cutting into the soil, forming rivulets and gullies, carrying soil down toward the stream banks. The action of water on the hillslopes over tens of thousands of years has exposed the previously enclosed tips of the lateral sheets which, piled one on top of another, form the ridge.

This exposed catena of soils—arranged in horizontal bands across the face of the hillslope, the bands with varying degrees of moisture and mineral content—provided the lineage of Nafa and their people a considerable range of soil types and climax vegetation within an extremely narrow zone—some thirty to fifty-five meters vertically (see Figure 1, a cross-sectional diagram of the hillslope). This differentiated environment permitted the agriculturalist to grow a wider range of food plants within a shorter distance of his compound than could be grown on the flatter surfaces at the top of the ridge. The eroded higher ground, less varied in soils exposed, held moisture less well, was more open to clearance by fire, tended to be less enclosed by woodland, was more open to the penetration of keepers of cattle and growers of grain seeking drier and more grassy land for habitation, herding, and cultivation. This is not to say that there were absolute differences between hillslope and ridge top or that there were clear demarcations between one and the other. The point is that the selection of the hillslopes by Nafa's people would have placed them within a marginally moister and somewhat more wooded zone, offering them access to wet soils on the valley floor for propagation of root crops, moist yet well drained soils on the mid-slopes for the cultivation of bananas and for the convenient harvest of firewood, and access to the slightly more open and grassy areas toward the crests of the ridge for the sowing and culti-vation of millet.

We know precious little about the daily lives of Nafa's people among the compounds and homes they established between the Nabisira and the Nakaibaale. We know the ap-

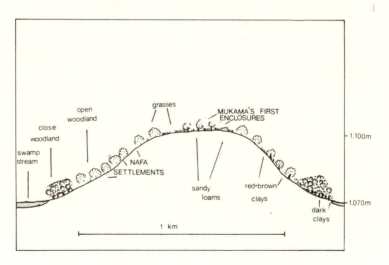

FIGURE 1 ● Cross-sectional Diagram of the Ridge at Bunafu, after David N. McMaster, *A Subsistence Crop Geography of Uganda*, pp. 3-7.

proximate locations of some eight or nine early compounds, and we know that they were located within an area of about four square miles. (See map 9.) They conformed to the patterns of settlement prevailing throughout this zone of Busoga in the present century, the residences scattered across the hillslope. There is no tradition of groups within the Busoga area living within compact or nucleated settlements, except as a measure of defense in the flatter and far more open lands of southeastern Busoga, Samia, and Bugwe, where people dug trenches and threw up walls around their concentrated settlements to protect themselves from raids from the east (and later from Buganda). Most Basoga lived in the past, and live today, in unfenced and scattered compounds hidden among the banana gardens upon which they are dependent for their food, for their beer, and for much of their building material. The dispersal of compounds optimizes the use of the varying soils up and down the hillslope. It provides a context for the emergence and maintenance of heroic traditions centered on the clearing of the land, and this in turn constitutes the basis for maintaining within the lineage of the clearer of the land, eternal rights to, and control over, the land. There is an enduring ideal that each man is master of his compound in the same sense that a king is master of his domain.[2] The common man's estate is an enclosed world, with or without fence; and within the boundary marking off his land, he is lord. His own principal house, wives' houses, and outbuildings are carefully sited around a courtyard in a form similar to that of the royal compound. The wives' houses and adjoining gardens are arranged according to their seniority within the compound. Barkcloth trees are planted not only to produce an important trade good—barkcloth—but also to mark the boundaries of the estate and to mark the sites of ancestral houses, now fallen down. A great barkcloth tree, the *mugaire gwa Kintu* is a focal point of the compound.

43

There, offerings are made for the protection of the household, and visitors gather to be entertained and to discuss the gossip of state, neighborhood, and family. And under that tree one notes styles of etiquette and respect for the master of the compound that are not dissimilar to those of the court.

But these are the ideals of a mature community. In fact, newcomers had to wrest clearings from the forest in order to begin planting. Brush had to be cut back and burned so as to destroy the habitats of bothersome flies and small animals. This was difficult work. The first fruits of cultivation would not provide the security sought. Nor would the second or the third. The first years of laborious penury would not permit one to attract wives for oneself or for one's sons, nor to attract followers, nor to engage servants, for there would be little surplus realizable in the beginning. So rather than entertaining in courtly compounds, the new settlers surely spent years holding back forest and bush. Instead of rejoicing in new found independence, the young man surely found it necessary to give himself over to bonds of dependence to master, in-law, and chief.[3] While difficult, these rough years of existence could give reality to the traditional ideal of using one's own labor to open up the land and thereby to establish within several generations rights to both the land and the elevated status that landedness accords.

The analysis of data drawn from traditions of migration and settlement suggests that when members of the lineage of Nafa established themselves on the Nabisira around the close of the eighteenth century, they placed themselves within a large and thinly occupied zone of central and northern Busoga. The zones of concentrated settlement in Luuka and Bugabula lay to the south and southwest. To the east, the Kigulu state had expanded little beyond the hills and moister lands of the south. To the northeast, the Bulamogi, Bukono, and Busiki states were organized around the control of lands lying adjacent to the

Mpologoma River. Beyond these more densely settled areas was a thinly occupied region, which was largely outside the range of regular administration—what might be termed an "unadministered zone." (See map 6.)

Nafa's community was one of perhaps a hundred small communities located within this unadministered zone. Among these were a few old settlements along the Nile River and along the Lake Kyoga shore, which constituted ferry points and controlled markets on the eastern frontier of a trade circuit centered on iron production and salt extraction in the lands of Bunyoro, several hundred kilometers west of Busoga. Other communities engaged the contacts of itinerant keepers of cattle whose mobility laced a network of continuing communication among the peoples of northern Busoga, of Kaberamaido (north of Lake Kyoga), of Pallisa to the northeast, and of Bugerere and Buruli (west of the Nile).

Still other communities in the unadministered zone were in fact the "colonies" of the administered core regions, weakly tethered settlements lying well beyond the regular borders. Other communities were organized around religious shrines and sacred places of greater than local importance. Some communities in the zone were simply places of refuge beyond the range of active control and discipline of the expanding states of central Busoga and beyond the reach of the pillaging armies of Buganda.

That these communities lay beyond the regular control of the developing political centers of Busoga does not mean that they were self-sustaining political and economic "capsules." We have, unfortunately, precious little data that illuminate the economic and political life of communities lying outside the areas of regular administration, but what we do know suggests that they were far from being autonomous entities. There were not, however, networks of regular markets and trade routes, these more formal chan-

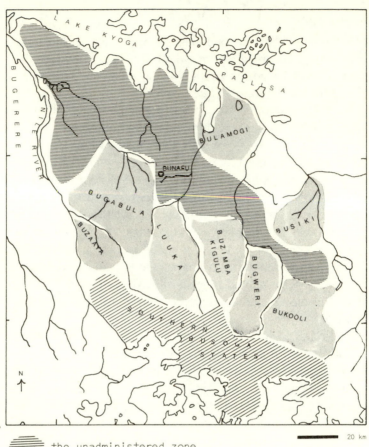

  the unadministered zone

  the regularly administered
zones of northern, central,
and eastern Soga states in
1800

  region of southern Soga
states

MAP 6 • The Unadministered Zone. At the close of the eighteenth century, a large region of what is today northern Busoga lay outside the spheres of regular administration. Nafa's community was one of perhaps a hundred small communities located within this unadministered zone.

46

nels of contact and exchange developing from west to east and from south to north only later in the nineteenth century. In 1800, the only regular markets in the region that is today Busoga were located in southern Busoga, oriented toward a Lake Victoria trade circuit; on the southern margins of the core regions of the northern states, again oriented toward the Lake Victoria traffic; and at collection and ferry points along the Nile River, the Lake Kyoga shoreline, and the Mpologoma River—oriented toward the northerly iron and salt trade from Bunyoro. It was only in the period between 1830 and 1860 that markets such as Nawaka and Kagulu became regular centers of exchange along expanding, intensifying, and regularized trade networks. (See map 17, chapter VII.)

If in the decades before the erection of Mukama's first enclosure north of the Nabisira, there were no regular markets and trade routes to draw off surpluses and to feed the requirements of the region's population, how were communities such as Nafa's able to gain access to goods and services they could not produce themselves? We have no explicit traditions or evocative data from Bunafu that expose the means by which Nafa's people were supplied with goods—such as finished and unfinished ironware, certain types of pottery, and various foodstuffs—that they almost certainly were unable to supply for themselves. Yet we can piece together a crude profile of the regional economy of the unadministered zone from evidence that refers to various parts of the region at different times. The profile draws upon observations of the great variety of exchange mechanisms that evidence indicates have been significant in areas of Busoga remote from regular administrative centers. And the profile is constructed with a strict chronological concern for traditions that hold the pasts of particular markets and trade "roads" to have been of indeterminate antiquity.

The profile offers a series of images of a regional econ-

47

omy of the unadministered zone in the early nineteenth century structured not upon the "channeled effect" associated with international and interregional trade but structured, rather, upon a remarkably extensive and thickly knit network of circulation, distribution, and redistribution. The images drawn suggest that even a small and isolated community could be supplied with goods and services that only specialists offered or that derived only from remote centers of extraction and manufacture.

What were these patterns of exchange by which goods and services circulated in this setting? There was, first, a relatively institutionalized exchange associated with the support of migration and pioneering. Sons setting off to establish themselves in a new place were given, or allowed to take, weapons, tools, food, live animals, skins, drums, pipes, seeds, nuts, shoots, tubers, and rhizomes. These few materials would make it possible for the migrant to establish his own food supply and to free himself quickly from conditions of extreme dependence or servitude in the new place. These portable goods would also lubricate his entrance into the new community, for certain of them could serve as gifts for his new masters and neighbors—to acquire status and land thereby.

Traditions also record that migrants could rely upon occasional help from relatives back home for a number of years, at least where proximity and political conditions made intermittent communication possible. Food, replacement tools, and live animals might be expected after a year or two. It would not have been exceptional for a second migrant to be sent along to join and assist his relative, bringing with him more goods—perhaps, too, a sister. Under the best conditions, patterns of regular communication and exchange were established between the primary and secondary settlements.

One can identify a second pattern of exchange, less

codified as custom in tradition than the transfer of goods associated with the support of migration and pioneering. Communities in the unadministered zone such as Nafa's did, over time, accumulate surplus produce—barkcloth, skins, and live animals. On an occasional basis, perhaps not even as frequently as once a year, parties transported these goods as far as thirty kilometers to exchange them for iron-ware, pottery, animals, and salt. The sites of such collective exchange were the eastern termini of the Bunyoro trade routes or, alternatively, more accessible villages which had themselves used the vehicle of occasional collective exchange to acquire valuable goods. The goods acquired would then be carried back to the village and distributed to the residents who had organized the venture.

Third, there were in the unadministered zone men and women who were specialist producers and craftsmen—blacksmiths, fishermen, potters. They were patronized by individuals who might travel as far as fifteen kilometers to obtain such goods as finished tools. Blacksmiths received used hoes, unfinished iron, and broken tools and weapons, as well as live animals, barkcloth, and foodstuffs, in exchange for finished metalware. Throughout the Lake Victoria region iron goods were continuously recycled. Ore extraction was undertaken at relatively few sites—along the Lake Victoria coast and in Bunyoro. Iron was then traded in the form of finished or unfinished hoe blades over long distances from smelting sites located at the points of extraction. These blades were then finished, if necessary, or converted to other metal goods close to the locations of use. By 1840, there were blacksmiths residing within nine kilometers of Nafa's community producing specialized weapons and tools. Forty years earlier, blacksmiths may not have been so close, but a few at least must have been accessible to Nafa's community.[4]

A fourth mechanism of circulation that can be identified

with the regional economy of the unadministered zone involved payments associated with ritual and with worship. As we shall see, the influence of the lineage of Nafa among the households established above the Nabisira was enhanced by Nafa's recognized ability to assign power to objects, to make charms and amulets, and to perform other services of a religious kind. Nafa's antecedents were ritual specialists in the court of Bukono to the northeast, and several members of related lineages who settled elsewhere performed like services. The ennobling qualities that lay behind these services were not offered freely. Payments were made in kind—foodstuffs, live animals, barkcloth, and skins—either to the person performing the services or as an offering at the shrine that Nafa's lineage maintained. Goods received were circulated among Nafa's lineage or were given as prestige goods to members of Nafa's community in return for tribute of food, drink, labor, loyalty, and song. And Nafa was but one of a number of ritual specialists—*bafumu* and *balaguzi*[5]—who lived among and served the population of the unadministered zone. The patronage of ritual services at crucial times of passage and at times of personal and group crisis would by itself ensure a constant and considerable circulation of goods and services.

Still another mechanism of circulation, and one of some importance, was theft. There are many references in the traditions of Busoga both to the raiding activities of various groups and individuals and to the difficulties of avoiding thievery while traveling. Several place-names in the unadministered zone are derived from references to the frequency of hijacking in those neighborhoods. Several men are glorified in tradition as thieves, and it is possible that some communities sustained themselves largely through brigandage, though the evidence here is very tangential. The large armies of dissidents, which developed in the unadministered forest zones of what is today eastern Buganda, certainly did sustain themselves in this way.

50

One might also place kidnapping in this category. Kidnapping appears to have been a common and continuous worry throughout Busoga from at least the end of the eighteenth century. The unadministered zone appears to have been a particularly attractive target of kidnappers seeking captives to transfer to Buganda. This zone was, for much of the nineteenth century, an important feeding ground for the long-distance trade in East Africa. The goods sought from the Lake Victoria region were, indeed, ivory and slaves. Later in the nineteenth century, a more diffuse pattern of collection based on occasional or itinerant kidnappers would be replaced by large-scale tribute taking and direct capture by armies of raiders from Soga states and from Buganda. In the sense that kidnappers were ultimately paid for their services, this too contributed to the velocity of circulation of goods and services in the region outside the direct control of the northern states.

A sixth, and rather more felicitous, mechanism by which goods and services in the region circulated involved the payment of "brideprice," which families demanded to secure the marriage contracts of their daughters. It is likely that at the close of the eighteenth century, brideprice in northern Busoga was offered in a mix of goods and services—new and used ironware, barkcloth, skins, live animals, salt, land, and labor. While brideprice is often spoken of as symbolic, it has in Africa reflected a monetary value—constructed in terms of the sorts of goods, services, and currencies of importance in everyday life and varying with changes in local and regional consumption and pricing. In Busoga, the goods paid over as brideprice would have been circulated through the lineage of the bride, with the understanding—in fact it is a highly durable contract—that if the marriage should break up a reasonably equivalent mix of goods would be returned to the lineage of the husband.

These are but six of the longer-range instruments by which the circulation of valuable goods and services was

51

sustained. There were others—donations, loans of materials, cattle bonds, visiting gifts, petty tribute, intrahouse-
hold exchanges—that still further extended and intensified
the networks of circulation. This profuse mix of exchange
institutions made possible the survival and growth of communities far from the termini of regular trade routes and
well outside the economies of the growing, but still small,
northern states.

This is a profile of the wider economic world within
which Nafa's small community was located, a profile built
up of images of a highly diffracted kind. Beyond this, the
collective memory of the people of the ridge today provides
little detail on the immediate world of Nafa's people. For
today's residents of the ridge, Nafa's epoch is placed at the
beginning of time, and Nafa is, at best, a one-dimensional
relic of a remote era. It is the new Mukama, not Nafa, who,
in the perceptions of the people of Bunafu, is seen to have
given motion and life to this area, who is continuous with,
and progenitor of, the present. With the elevation to dominance of the lineage of the new Mukama, a great new family descended from King Wambuzi of Luuka and from
Mukanni would flow around the eastern end of the ridge,
and the experience of Nafa and his people would dissolve to
the background in the traditions of the people of the area.
Beyond the ridge, however, in the lands from which Nafa's
people came and in the lands to which many of his followers
fled, there is evidence to be found that permits a somewhat
broader glimpse of Nafa's immediate world at the time of
Mukama's birth.

There are ten lineages whose traditions carry them back
to the core of Nafa's community above the Nabisira in the
years just before the erection of an enclosure for Mukama
above Nafa's settlements. These traditions taken together
indicate that Nafa's world was something of a refuge for
families and individuals fleeing the expansion of the Luuka

state, particularly for families fleeing the expanding Luuka
state during the reign of Inhensiko I, the second ruler of
Luuka. Inhensiko I granted *mitala* "estates" to his sixteen
sons. The *mitala* (sing. *mutala*) were sections of raised land
defined, typically, by the streams or swamps that transected
the landscape and, as has been seen, provided natural
boundaries for the subdivisions of the state. In the Luuka
area these naturally demarcated *mitala* ranged from four to
twenty square kilometers. In the late 1880s there were approximately 105 *mitala* within the area described by the
kingdom of Luuka at the time. Bunafu, Makutu, Nsambya,
and Nasumiti are today *mitala* and were at the close of the
nineteenth century among the *mitala* estates that comprised
the domain of Luuka.

The granting of the *mitala* estates to the sixteen sons of
Inhensiko I was one generator of the rapid expansion of the
Luuka state that took place during Inhensiko's reign. The
other important component of this expansive process was
the installation of trusted commoners in chiefly offices of
greater authority than the *mitala* positions. These upper-
level officials were responsible for the collection of tribute,
the expansion of the domain, and the oversight of princes
and of the *mitala* estates that the sons of the ruler and their
descendants had been granted. In several senses, these appointments meant that Inhensiko was "the owner of the
land." It was in taking control of the "land," both in his
own right and through the investiture of his sons, that Inhensiko made his presence felt by the preexisting communities of settlers. The installation of a prince on a ridge
transformed the nature of social relations among the groups
settled there. It was not merely a case of a faraway major-
domo to whom gifts were to be sent on occasion. The
prince, entering the community with new ideas of his own
cultural distinctiveness and innate political and social su-
periority, shattered existing ideas about dominance and so-

53

cial control based on prior residence, land clearance, and leadership seasoned in experience. Many groups could not stand the changes fomented by the arrival of a prince. Many, too, were not tolerated by the prince and his close retinue. This discordance between old and new, so heavily felt during the long reign of Inhensiko I, caused a steady flight of families from the zones of expansion. Some fled west to more open lands in the Bugabula area, some fled north across the Nabisira. Of the ten lineages we can place within the small domain of Nafa at about the time of the erection of Mukanni's shelter, five had fled the expanding Luuka state during Inhensiko I's reign. Significantly, perhaps, four of these refugee groups had still earlier come from the far south, twenty to fifty kilometers beyond the southern boundary of Luuka, from close to the northern coast of Lake Victoria. (See map 7.)

Of these four groups that both fled Luuka and trace their origins back to the Lake Victoria coast, two are sections of the Maganda clan. These Maganda lineages are of the Lungfish totem and are part of the great stream of Lungfish groups that spread along the northern shores of Lake Victoria and through most of the Buganda kingdom from a number of points of dispersal around the northern coasts of Lake Victoria.[6] The Maganda folk who reached the Nabisira had fled Nasumiti just a few kilometers to the east of Nafa's community. It was at Nasumiti that Inhensiko I had installed Kalalu, a commoner of the Muluuta clan, as a first step in the expansion of the Luuka state north of the Nabisira.

One lineage of another lacustrine clan found its way into Nafa's world, and here too after a flight from Inhensiko's Luuka. This was Naguha's family of the Kabambwe clan. The Kabambwe are of the Reedbuck totem and, like the lineages of the Maganda clan, had spread through the islands and coastlands along the northern shores of Lake Vic-

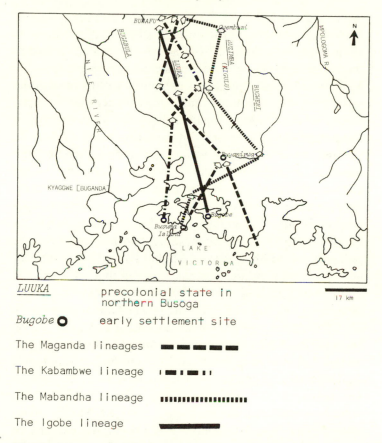

LUUKA   precolonial state in
                         northern Busoga   17 km

Bugobe ⦿   early settlement site

The Maganda lineages   ▬ ▬ ▬ ▬ ▬

The Kabambwe lineage   ▪ ▬ ▪ ▬ ▪▪

The Mabandha lineage   ▪▪▪▪▪▪▪▪▪▪▪▪▪▪▪▪

The Igobe lineage   ▬▬▬▬▬

MAP 7 ● From the Lakeshore. At the time young Mukama arrived on the
ridge above Nafa's lands, there were established on the hillslope five patrilineages that had once lived near the northern coast of Lake Victoria.
The migrations of these groups from lacustrine residences to Bunafu were
neither rapid nor simple. A number of intervening "stops" were, in fact,
occupied for long periods. The mapping of the movements shown here is
notional. The segmentations of groups, many of the intervening sites of
occupation, and the number of generations are passed over in this
simplified reconstruction. The two Maganda lineages are represented as
one.

55

toria, apparently before the foundation of the kingdom of Buganda some six centuries ago. While the Lungfish groups appear to have expanded from an earlier area of settlement on the eastern side of the lake, the Reedbuck groups—the available evidence suggests—expanded from the opposite side, from the lakeshore zone lying between the Sesse Islands and the western Uganda grasslands. More recently—some three generations before the seating of Inhensiko I on the throne of Luuka—several Kabambwe families left Igemero, a settlement located on Buvuma Island in the northern waters of Lake Victoria. In a series of short migrations, sections of these lineages planted settlements along a northward track extending from the Luuka Hills to the Lumbuye River. Some of these settlements fell under the influence of the first rulers of Luuka: Nhiro and his son Inhensiko. It was during Inhensiko's reign that a Kabambwe family under the leadership of Naguha fled settlements close to the king's palace at Kiroba and reached the northern bank of the Nabisira, putting itself beyond the control of the Luuka ruler. Kabambwe groups established homes at Inula and at Ikumbya both lying north of the Nafa community, and at Bunafu, on the lowest and most southerly land within the range of Nafa's authority.[7]

Still another lacustrine lineage reached Nafa's world after a flight from Inhensiko. This was Kirevu's family of the Igobe clan. The Igobe clan is of the *Mpindi* totem, the *mpindi* being a small edible pea. The most prominent lineage of the Igobe clan had provided the rulers of the small Bugobe state in South Busoga. The ancestors of the princely family of Bugobe reached the northern coast of Lake Victoria more than five centuries ago as part of the expansion of *Mpindi* groups from the east, from the lands between Mount Elgon and the Lake Victoria shore. Several *Mpindi* states were established in South Busoga, and though we know little of their pasts, Bugobe appears to have been the weakest,

56

being accessible both to attacks from the sea and to expansionist adventurers from the interior. From around the beginning of the seventeenth century, fleets of raiders from the islands of Lake Victoria began harrassing the coastal trading communities, which were already under pressure from the expanding states in the interior of southern Busoga. The ensuing convulsions sent groups of refugees fleeing eastward and northward.[8] Igobe's family reached Budhabangula in the center of what was then Luuka, having carried to the north drumbeats, traditions, and other relics of their once royal status. Within another generation, Igobe's son Kirevu had left the Luuka domain following the installation of a son of Inhensiko I as the head of Budhabangula *mutala*. Kirevu migrated with his kin across the Nabisira and established a new home close to Nafa's.[9] It was Kirevu's son Kisodi who was the father of the young girl named Mukanni who went to King Wambuzi's palace.

These, then, were the four lacustrine groups, refugees from Inhensiko's program of political expansion, who reached Nafa's lands, all of them arriving there in the last decades of the eighteenth century and in the first decades of the nineteenth. There is a fifth group—Kamuse's lineage of the Mabandha clan—whose traditions carry them back to a Lake Victoria settlement but not to a flight from Luuka. At least one lineage of the Mabandha clan had traveled from southern Busoga in the early eighteenth century, reaching the northern frontier of the emerging Kigulu state, just east of Luuka. There, these Mabandha folk established a settlement at Gwembuzi. It was from Gwembuzi that Kamuse, a grandson of the founder of the Mabandha settlement there, traveled some fifteen kilometers to the west and established himself within Nafa's community. Kamuse's settlement appears to have been but one component of a steady expansion of Mabandha people westward from Gwembuzi right across Luuka and Bugabula.[10]

There was a sixth family—Wagubona's of the Mulondo clan—that fled Luuka proper during the expansive era of Inhensiko I. However, Wagubona's antecedents came not from the shores of Lake Victoria but rather from west of the Nile in what is today eastern Buganda. Wagubona's father, Chuka, with many others of his clan, fled settlements in eastern Buganda in the late eighteenth or early nineteenth century.We know that late eighteenth-century eastern Buganda—or that region just to the west of the Nile which the Ganda court was attempting to integrate securely in the domain—was marked by a number of significant disturbances. This was an area in which there were still strong interests on the part of representatives of the Nyoro court, and Bunyoro was at the time Buganda's major adversary. Moreover, the forests and swamps of this region had become refuges for Ganda dissidents and for princes attempting to assemble enough power to seize the Ganda throne. Semakokiro launched a successful revolt against his brother, Kabaka Junju, from the forests, demonstrating that these retreats were more than just the sanctuaries of brigands. Semakokiro's son Kakungulu attempted to build support in the forest for the overthrow of Kabaka Kamanya, who had succeeded Semakokiro as king of Buganda. The mother of Prince Kakungulu came from this region. Her family was large and important there and gave considerable support to, first, Semakokiro and, later, their son Kakungulu. (See figure 2, a simplified genealogy of the Kabakas of Buganda from approximately the beginning of the eighteenth century to the middle of the nineteenth century.) As supporters and parents of this great rebel, the lineages of the Monkey clan in the region were vulnerable to selective attacks by armies and parties both from the capital and from Kamanya's lieutenants in the field. From the beginning of Kamanya's reign, Monkey clan settlements were being viciously sacked. Victims of these campaigns fled to more

remote refuges east of the Nile. One of these sackings at
Kalebera sent Chuka, the Mulondo man of the Monkey to-
tem, flying to the east. He settled for a short time at Luwoko
Hill in southern Luuka and later went to Buwologoma.
(See map 2 in the introduction.)

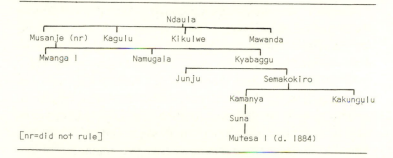

FIGURE 2 ● A Simplified Genealogy of the Kabakas of Buganda from the
Beginning of the 18th Century.

It was from Buwologoma that Chuka's son Wagubona
migrated north. Nafa's community would have presented
some attractions to Wagubona. First, it was a community of
refuge beyond the borders of Luuka, occupied by a number
of families, some of whom had arrived seeking refuge. Second, it was located within several kilometers of two communities in which there were families of the Monkey totem
whose antecedents had fled Buganda. Third, Nafa must
have credited the Mulondo with some worth, for he gave
Wagubona not only land upon which to settle but also his
daughter Lubagu to marry.

There were people of at least four other lineages residing
within the province of Nafa's authority at the time of the
birth of Mukama. These four groups were neither refugees
from the expansion of the Luuka state nor migrants from the
coast. Two of the lineages represented were of what is today
called the Nangwe clan, and they appear to have traveled

but a very short distance from the north to reach Bunafu. The third was Bawutu's lineage of the Mwebya clan, and the fourth was Nafa's lineage of the Muganza clan, these last two having come from the northeast, from the Mpologoma River area on the eastern side of modern Busoga. (See map 8.)

The two Nangwe lineages both trace their descent from a figure named Kibuli who lived north of the Nabisira before the foundation of the Luuka state.[11] These descendants of Kibuli were the only "pre-Nafa" settlers who can be identified within the area between the Nakaibaale and the northwest arm of the Nabisira. Today, the Nangwe clan is an enormously large group, perhaps the largest clan never having held the rulership of a Busoga state.[12] They are today of the Mushroom totem, yet at the beginning of the twentieth century there were some twenty groups in Busoga having as totem one or another finely distinguished species of mushroom. In clan meetings held during this century at various places across Busoga, these groups sought to unify themselves. Today, all groups in Busoga of the Mushroom totem are called Nangwe, or Mulumba-Nangwe, the Nangwe name superimposed on all of the various clan eponyms that were previously used as identification. The elders who participated in these meetings speak of the intent as reunification, though the thesis that all Nangwe subclans and lineages are related historically is problematic. What is clear is that Mushroom families were settled at scores of sites within the Busoga area at the time of the foundation of the northern Busoga states. An attractive and entirely speculative hypothesis is that the finely differentiated Mushroom totems within the narrow range of Busoga denote an intense interest in forage foods. This, in turn, suggests the possibility that the Mushroom or Nangwe groups were among the gathering peoples surviving in Busoga from an early time, peoples who preceded the appearance of agriculture in the

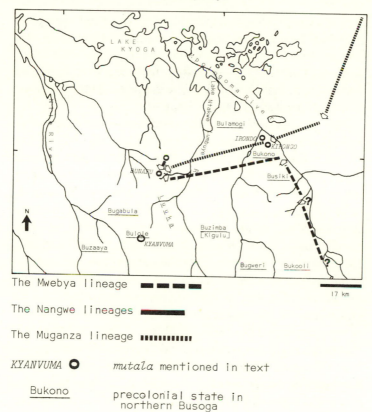

The Mwebya lineage ▬ ▬ ▬ ▬

The Nangwe lineages ▬▬▬▬

The Muganza lineage ▪▪▪▪▪▪▪▪▪▪

KYANVUMA ⬤   *mutala* mentioned in text

<u>Bukono</u>   precolonial state in
northern Busoga

MAP 8 ● The Other Migrants. There were four other lineages established
within Nafa's world when young Mukama arrived on the ridge at Bunafu.
There was Bawutu's lineage of the Mwebya clan. There were the
lineages of Kibuli of the Nangwe clan which apparently predated Nafa in
the region immediately north of the Nabisira River. And there was of
course Nafa's own lineage. Curiously, segments of all these three clans
were in close contact on the Mpologoma River in Bukono, and all three
were in close contact at the Kyanvuma shrine in Bulole (located south of
Bunafu). And all were in close contact at Bunafu. The representations of
migrational routes are notional. The movements of the Mwebya lineages
along the Mpologoma River are extremely difficult to detail. The Nangwe
lineages at Bunafu trace their "origins" to the immediate vicinity of
Bunafu. Many Nangwe groups were established along the Mpologoma
River before the end of the eighteenth century.

61

region some two to three thousand years ago and were present when Bantu-speaking people expanded through the region at a period roughly contemporaneous with the introduction of agriculture and who, in time, were absorbed within the agricultural and Bantu-speaking groups that established themselves among them.

Two groups remain to be discussed—the lineage of Bawutu of the Mwebya clan and lineage of Nafa of the Muganza clan. Members of Bawutu's lineage reached Nafa's settlement above the Nabisira in the generation preceding Inhensiko's reign. The various Mwebya lineages of the *Namukenhe* fish totem are superficially a group of common kinship, but the traditions of the Mwebya lineages point to quite varied places of dispersal, routes of migration, and timings of entry into the general area of Busoga. Some lineage members today point to origins in the northeast corner of Lake Victoria, dispersing from there up the Mpologoma River system as far as Lake Kyoga. Others point to origins in the central Mpologoma area, in the environs of the early Bukono and Busiki states. Still others point to the Buvuma Islands and to central Kyaggwe (eastern Buganda) as earlier zones of settlement and dispersal. It is possible that one core *Namukenhe* group did break up along the Mpologoma River—virtually all *Namukenhe* groups in Busoga today have traditions pointing to origins along the Mpologoma. In fact, the arteries of the Mpologoma offer a geographical context for the rapid segmentation of kin groups within a relatively small space. Many lineages in Busoga today trace their movements back through time and space to residences built upon floating papyrus islands in the Mpologoma River system. This "floating population" is referred to by the more firmly grounded peoples of the area as the *Bakenyi* or *Bakenhe*,[13] Some Mwebya Bakenhe left such floating existences and traveled to the west, some settling in Busoga, others reaching as far as eastern Buganda on the other side of the Nile.

There is another tradition that traces the Mwebya lineages back to Kyanvuma in the small Bulole state just west of Luuka. Kyanvuma was, clearly, a secondary point of "origin" for many Mwebya families in Bugabula, Luuka, Bulamogi, and Busiki—a pinion for migrational stories referring to the recent past. Kyanvuma is said by some to have been the principal clan shrine of the Mwebya lineages, but what is interesting is that the tradition of the Kyanvuma shrine, along with other evidence, knits together many Mwebya families with families of the Muganza clan of Nafa and with families associating themselves today with the Nangwe clan.[14] Both of these clans—Muganza and Nangwe—maintain important clan shrines at Kyanvuma in Bulole, but they also maintain traditions of association with an earlier Kyanvuma shrine in Bukono in northeast Busoga. This Bukono shrine was itself controlled by a parent Muganza lineage. What is suggested here is an enduring association among several lineages of the Mwebya, Muganza, and Nangwe groups extending from early settlements in Bukono along the Mpologoma westward to later settlements at Bulole to the west of Luuka. Comigration and perhaps preferred marriage arrangements contributed to the maintenance of relationships amidst widespread dispersals of descendants over many generations. It was also within Nafa's small community that segments of the same lineages were represented. Here, as in Bukono, the Muganza lineage appears to have carried precedence within the close-knit nexus of relations among the three groups.

The Muganza clan, to which Nafa's lineage belongs, are of the *Kaduyu* totem (the *Hyrax* or rockrabbit), and the origin traditions of the several *Kaduyu* groups in the Busoga area carry them back to a common region of "origin" to the east of the Mpologoma River across from Bukono and Busiki. There, the traditions record, the Muganza group was settled at a site named for the Iganza shrine located there. And it was in this area that Muganza families began to capitalize on deeper relationships with Lwo-speaking hunters and cattle keepers living close by in temporary camps. Some ten generations ago, Muganza men and women along with Lwo-speaking folk began to cross the Mpologoma, establishing new camps just above the marsh that marks the western side of the river. Muganza families ultimately settled at Irondo and Kirongo, very close to what would become the sites of the first capitals of the Lwo rulers of Bukono.[15] Within the Bukono state, they were accorded high status as "Baganza," those "annointed with favored status." And there, the Muganza families made what the evidence suggests were the first of what would be enduring relationships with Mwebya and Nangwe groups settled on the western banks of the Mpologoma.[16]

The antecedents of the Nafa figure of Bunafu, these early Baganza in Bukono are an interesting group. The available evidence suggests that the Muganza group was not origi- nally Bantu speaking, that the Muganza group was at an ear- lier date known by a different name, that the Muganza name emerged amidst contacts on the western side of the Mpologoma as the Lwo founders of the Bukono state came to be absorbed within a Bantu-speaking world, that the close association between the Muganza group and Lwo speakers prevailed at a considerably earlier period and at lo- cations geographically remote from Busoga, and, last, that the Muganza group was a component of the deepest exten- sion of Paranilotic peoples southward through the region be- tween Mount Elgon and Lake Kyoga.

The first indication comes from the *baiwa* (sing. *mwiwa*) names, which the Muganza people today maintain. The *baiwa* are the children of the daughters of the clan, not technically members of the clan but intimately associated with it through combination of obligations and rights exist- ing between these "children" and members of their mother's patrilineage and clan. Clans in Busoga today have a special name they accord to all their *baiwa*, of whatever clan affiliations they may be. These *baiwa* names are occasionally useful in attempting to reconstruct the past, for they may unveil a still earlier clan identity, through a name that evokes or suggests wider associations.

For the Muganza clan, the name given to female *baiwa* is *Namuganza*. The name given to male *baiwa* is *Kalimo*. It is this *Kalimo* name that commands interest here, for there is a *Kalimo* clan in Busoga that is found mainly in Bukono and Bulamogi in northeast Busoga. It appears to have been associated in the past with the Muganza clan. To the east of Busoga, this *Kalimo* clan is also present, though it is occasionally known as the *Kadimo*. This is not a different name, merely one that reflects an extremely common sound change when moving from one dialect of Bantu speech to another. The *Kadimo* of eastern Uganda maintain traditions that retrace their settlements to several sites east of the Mpologoma also recalled by the Muganza people of Busoga.

But the *Kalimo* or *Kadimo* name pushes back in time and northward in direction the "earlier origins" of the Muganza group. The *Kadimo* or *Kalimo* name may associate the Muganza group of Busoga with the *Kadimo* or *Jimos* "Agricultural Paranilotics" living in the hills of Karamoja in northeast Uganda some four centuries ago. In the regions of Najie, Nyakwai, and eastern Acholi in northern Uganda, these *Kadimo* were firemakers. They drew prestige and authority from their control of religious and ritual symbols and activities, such as kindling the "new fire."[17] Over several centuries the *Kadimo* of northern Uganda underwent considerable segmentation or fission, and groups left what is today the region of Karamoja in search of new places of settlement throughout—historians of northern Uganda tell us— the northeast quadrant of what is today Uganda. At various points and moments the *Kadimo* forged close relationships

65

with Lwo-speaking groups, and Lwo cultural forms and ideas were absorbed within the ritual of the *Kadimo* firemakers.[18]

In Busoga, the Muganza group is particularly and exceptionally associated with the ritual preservation and ritual re-kindling of fire. Even as recent a figure as Nafa—who appears in the context of the early nineteenth century to be Bantu speaking and who is recorded as having given up the production of sorghum and millet (the staples of *Kadimo* folk in eastern and northern Uganda)—gives fire to his followers in Bunafu.[19] Traditions of giving fire are rare among the aggregate traditions of Busoga, underscoring, perhaps, the exceptional position of Nafa among the Bantu-speaking population of the region. Moreover, like the *Kadimo* of northern Uganda, the Muganza figures were in a number of settings ritual specialists of some prestige. They appear to have gained influence among the peoples of Bukono through control of the Kyanvuma shrine.[20] They are re-called, too, as having been ritual specialists at the court of the ruler of Bukono. Muganza folk who migrated to the west, reaching the Bulole area west of Luuka, came to take a position of precedence among Nangwe and Mwebya groups through control of the Kyanvuma shrine. And just north of the Nabisira, Nafa parlayed the same ritual power and religious knowledge into a style of domination within the small community of Bunafu. The *Kadimo* name then, with the evidence relating to shrines, ritual, firemaking, and migration, suggests that the movement of Nafa into the area of Bunafu constituted one of the farthest extensions of once Paranilotic-speaking peoples southward.

Nafa, with a few followers, left Bukono some time during the last quarter of the eighteenth century. The traditions that relate this exodus suggest nothing about why Nafa left Bukono. But they do make clear that Nafa was neither the first nor the last of the "Baganza" to leave Bukono. The

Muganza folk who reached Kyanvuma in Bulole arrived there several generations before Nafa reached Bunafu. Later, other men of the Muganza clan—Ibengo, Wagabaza, and Mutagaya—left Bukono with a few followers and followed roughly the same tracks as Nafa and his predecessors, but traveled twenty kilometers farther west, reaching the capital of the ruler of the Bugabula kingdom some years after Nafa reached the Nabisira.

The detail in tradition that exposes the timing and direction of migrations is thick and tedious. The intent here in sketching the outlines of the migrations that brought various groups to the hillslope above the Nabisira derives not only from an antiquarian interest in the origins of groups. More importantly, the records of these migrations expose the remarkable diversity of experience and world that fell within the authority of Nafa's lineage. In precolonial eastern and central Africa, migration was the outstanding mode of social and cultural communication, the means by which knowledge flowed from one part of the continent to another, by which ideas filtered from community to community. Migration, in this sense, is not merely an appurtenance of tradition, it is a *force*. For Nafa's community, this complex, tedious record of migration reveals that located close to one another on a hillslope above the Nabisira were, in 1830, individuals whose antecedents had resided on the floating papyrus islands of the Mpologoma River system, had fished in and traded across Lake Victoria waters, had managed an environment offering 140 centimeters of rainfall per year and one providing but sixty, had carried the status of members of the ruling family of a small state, had participated in a movement to overthrow the king of Buganda, had been pillaged by an army from the capital of Buganda, had crossed the Nile, had empowered charms and amulets for the rulers of the Bukono state, had resided immediately next to the courts of kings as well as in worlds without kings, and had experienced a loss of place amidst the expansion of the Luuka state (see map 9).

One can only speculate on the processes by which day-to-day transactions among such a diverse congregation of people came to be possible. While of diverse origin, virtu-

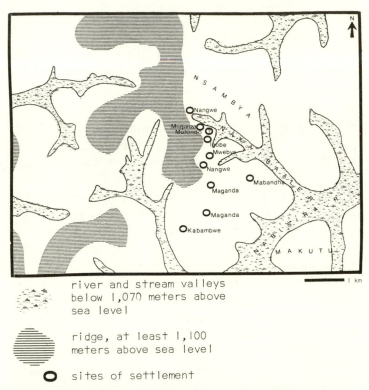

river and stream valleys
below 1,070 meters above
sea level

ridge, at least 1,100
meters above sea level

O   sites of settlement

MAP 9 • Early Settlements within Nafa's Community. At the time of arrival of young Mukama on the ridge above Nafa's compound, some ten lineages were established on the hillslopes above the Nabisira and Nakaibaale valleys. The map indicates the approximate location of the core settlement of each lineage group. Note that the location given for the Mulondo lineage is only a guess. Two lineages of the Maganda clan and two lineages of the Nangwe clan were present before the movement of Mukama to the ridge. In all cases, the lineage groups are identified by the clan names.

68

ally all would have shared a heightened valuation of security, refuge. They all, certainly, shared one member of Nafa's lineage as leader, as focal point of the community. We know through the evidence of marriage that the members of the various lineages came to be quickly linked socially and contractually in a network of marriages. They very likely shared a reasonably common status in respect to the control of land, all of them settling above the Nabisira within a period of approximately two generations, thereby giving no group absolute priority on the basis of an exceptionally old claim to the land. They all shared a common challenge in the activities of keepers of cattle and settlers higher up the ridge to the northwest. All shared a singular position in respect to the residence of the mothers of King Wambuzi. All shared a concern, perhaps, for the intentions of the Muluuta people—representatives of King Inhensiko I and then Wambuzi—stationed only several kilometers down the Nabisira. And they would share much greater challenges in the person of the young Mukama for whom a great enclosure was built on the flatter land of the ridge to the north and in the conflict that would eventually open up between Nafa's and Mukama's nodes of authority.

The community that had formed around Nafa's lineage by 1830 was rather different from many of the communities of the unadministered zone. Here, a useful distinction may be drawn between a "new community" like Nafa's, composed largely of individuals associated with lineages represented in the community for no more than two generations, and an "old community," in which most residents belonged to lineages present for at least three generations.

In his remarkable study of twentieth-century Busoga,[21] Lloyd A. Fallers drew just such a distinction between two types of community, one of which he termed "stable" (the old) and the other "broken network" (the new), which he saw as far less demographically stable. Working from his observations of several communities in the 1950s, Fallers saw the broken network evidenced in situations of extreme modernization, such as in the vicinity of new towns and in areas opened to resettlement after population removal associated with sleeping-sickness eradication programs. In the broken-network setting, high rates of population mobility would bring individuals of many lineages into a single village. The lineage groups would tend to be small, and any individual would have few or no lineage mates upon whom to rely.[22] Institutions structured upon lineage membership and lineage regulation, such as land holding and inheritance, would be severely weakened. "Kinship institutions," wrote Fallers about these circumstances, would "operate with less consistency."[23] The nature of regular social interaction would, for each individual, change. "The motivation to follow lineage norms . . . [would] tend to atrophy in the person who seldom sees his lineage-mates. Though it may be technically possible for him to maintain interaction with them, he . . . [would] tend rather to be influenced by the easier and more frequent contacts which he has with his non-kin neighbours." Fallers observed that the individual, given this, would have to "make other arrangements."[24]

Among the more remarkable changes that Fallers saw occurring in the unstable or broken-network community were a "decline in the position of older men," a decline in the rate of polygyny, a heightened mobility of sons in the next generation, a depreciation in the religious or sacred value of land, a decline in the "position of men in general *vis-a-vis* women," a rise in the frequency of divorce, a growth in importance of affinal links within the community and an obverse decline in the importance of patrilineal ties, and a surge of new forms of association based on pseudokinship or built upon new religious sects.[25] Fallers based his observations on statistical data, though one may also see the rather mechanical and predictable relationships between a new, young, and diverse population on the one hand and all other aspects of structure on the other.

As noted, Fallers traced the variations in demography, values, and social organization to differences in the degree of hetrogeneity of lineage composition in the Busoga community. In turn, the high levels of heterogeneity he observed in some communities were attributed to the modernizing forces of the twentieth century. But the observation of nineteenth-century communities such as Nafa's makes clear that comparable degrees of heterogeneity could be "achieved" by other means or as a consequence of other forces. Nafa's community, like Fallers' modernizing community, was composed of members of many unrelated lineages of diverse origins and recent arrival. It was a new community in the sense that those groups we can locate within the community around 1830 had arrived only in the previous generation or two. Lineage groups would have been extraordinarily shallow, a few members of one or two generations represented at most. As with the modernizing community, most social interaction would have been largely outside one's own kin group. The quality of relationships between and among individuals of different lineages would have been far more critical than those within lineages. In these important respects, Nafa's small community almost certainly resembled the broken-network communities Fallers found emerging around towns, at crossroads, and in the areas reopened to settlement after the sleeping-sickness epidemic of the early twentieth century.

We have no data on the numbers or statuses of older men relative to younger men in the community, no data on the rates of polygyny, no data on the relative statuses of men and women, and none on the frequency of divorce. There are, on the other hand, indications that affinal associations were, in Nafa's community, of exceptional significance in social relations and that young men remained relatively mobile both geographically and politically.

In regard to the character and structure of association, the evidence from Bunafu is still more firm. Bunafu became a context for the elaboration of forms of association, which, though not wholly new, were of a kind only rarely achieved in the wider Lake Victoria world. First Nafa and later Mukama Womunafu were at the center of complexes of ideas that accented ritual power, spirit possession, and separation from the formal political world. These ideas were assembled largely through migration into functioning institutions that would last more than a century beyond that moment when the young Mukama, son of King Wambuzi and Mukanni, was transferred to the new enclosure erected upon the ridge above Nafa's compound.

III

The Young Mukama

SEVERAL years after Mukanni's child was brought out of the house at Makutu, a large army from Buganda crossed the Nile into southwest Busoga. For over a century, Ganda armies had intermittently raided and for all intents and purposes reduced to submission the small states lying within about fifteen kilometers of present-day Jinja at the Nile outlet of Lake Victoria. Ganda adventurers had been seeking for decades to make their careers in combat in Busoga, hoping to carry back to the courts of Buganda tales of victory and headloads of booty. By the middle of Kabaka Kamanya's reign—and he ruled from approximately 1805-1836[1]—Ganda armies had expanded their horizons to the western banks of the Kiko River, and Kamanya had become the first Ganda king to receive regular tribute from the southern Busoga states. The tribute, paid in meat, dried bananas (*mutere*), beer, crafts, and women, flowed into the center of Buganda through the court of the Ssekiboobo, the chief of Kyaggwe. Kyaggwe was the most eastern province of Buganda, and the office of Ssekiboobo would, right through the nineteenth century, supervise Buganda's expanding hegemony to the east of the Nile. (See map 10.)

While Ganda control was firmly established in the area of Jinja by the early nineteenth century, the kingdom's activities reached only to the Kiko River. And while the crossing of the Nile near Jinja had for the Baganda become routine, down river beyond the Budhagali Falls the influence of the Ganda kings was weak. This region north of the Budhagali Falls, encompassing open lands and forest on both sides of the Nile, was a crucial one, an area of endur-

73

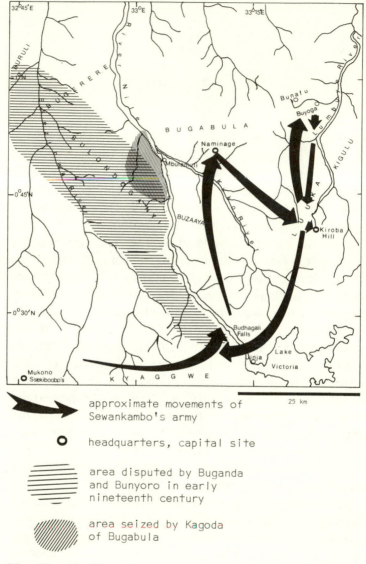

approximate movements of
Sewankambo's army

○ headquarters, capital site

area disputed by Buganda
and Bunyoro in early
nineteenth century

area seized by Kagoda
of Bugabula

25 km

MAP 10 ● The Ekyetoloolo Campaign. During the reign of Kabaka
Kamanya of Buganda, a major Ganda campaign was mounted to the east
against the Bugabula and Luuka kingdoms. The Ganda army, directed by
Ssekiboobo Sewankambo of Kyaggwe region of Buganda, crossed the
Nile near present-day Jinja and passed north toward Kagoda's capital at
Naminage. The army crossed the wide Kiko River and burned Naminage
and then moved to Luuka where Wambuzi's capital at Kiroba Hill was
burned. The army then moved north, but stopped at Buyoga, to the west
of the Lumbuye River, before turning south again and marching back to
Buganda.

ing conflict between the Buganda and Bunyoro kingdoms over two centuries. While the area was much closer to the Ganda capitals than to those of Bunyoro, the great Ssezibwa Swamp cuts a wide swath through the land from north to south, making access difficult between the center of Buganda and the region north of Budhagali. This was the far frontier of the kingdom of Bunyoro. Pastoralists and cultivators oriented toward the Nyoro throne pushed into the lands of Buruli, Bugerere, and northern Kyaggwe, just as they had moved into northern Busoga east of the Nile. These groups pressed south establishing communities oriented toward the Nyoro throne.

It was in the eighteenth century that this zone north of Budhagali became a region of contention and then of open conflict between Ganda and Nyoro states. Armies of the two kingdoms faced one another many times over the issue of this distant eastern frontier. But it was more than a Nyoro presence to their east that worried the councilors of Buganda in the eighteenth century. This eastern area was, as has been noted, also a zone of refuge for dissident Baganda. Contentious Ganda princes were, with exasperating regularity, removing themselves to this protected region amidst swamp and forest to build forces for the overthrow of the reigning king. There can be no doubt that members of the Ganda court saw these revolts as alliances with the Nyoro kingdom, and occasionally this perception may have been correct. In any event, Ganda campaigns to the east were virtually always double pronged and of first priority.

It was Semakokiro, Kabaka Kamanya's predecessor, who seems to have been the first Ganda prince to mount a successful revolt from the forests of Kyaggwe. It was there that Semakokiro built his forces and subsequently attacked and overthrew his brother, Kabaka Junju. A generation later, Semakokiro's son Kakungulu pursued a similar revolt against Kamanya from the same refuge. But Kakungulu—

who had had an earlier career in the east assisting his
father's campaign against Junju—took his revolt one step
further and moved into open alliance with the Nyoro king of
the day, Kyebambe Namatukula. Much of Kamanya's long
reign was consumed by warfare with Bunyoro and with
Prince Kakungulu.[2]

Given the situation, it could hardly have been expected
that Soga states just to the east of the Nile would long remain outside this large and many-fronted conflict. During
the reign of Kamanya, Kagoda, the ruler of Bugabula, made
a bold move across the Nile. In the first phase, this involved
raiding the area of Bulondoganyi, but then Kagoda sent
settlers across the Nile and seized the important ferry point
across from Mbulamuti. (See map 10.) This move both
strengthened and made more overt an older alliance with
Bunyoro. For Kakungulu, this enhancement of an alliance
on the eastern flank of Buganda was of crucial importance.
With a strong ally along the Nile, Kakungulu himself could
proceed to make new initiatives on the northern and northwest margins of the Buganda kingdom. Kagoda would hold
the old eastern stronghold, and Kakungulu, with Nyoro assistance, would take his campaign of harrassment to other
border zones.

Thus when Ssekiboobo Sewankambo crossed the Nile at
the head of a large army, the success of his campaign was
more crucial to the survival of Kabaka Kamanya than any
previous campaign to the east. The Ganda army did not attack Bugabula directly, but rather crossed the Nile at its
own ferry point near Jinja. From there, it moved through the
tribute states of southwestern Busoga, and then pressed
northeastward in the direction of Kagoda's capital at
Naminage.

There was good reason why the Kiko River had constituted the horizon of Ganda activity in Busoga for more than
a generation, why the lands to the east and north of the Kiko

had been untouched by Ganda imperialism. The Kiko River is a broad swamp. Its normal expanse would have been a considerable obstacle to the advance of a large army. The crossing of the Kiko River on this occasion suggests not only a change in strategy, but also in the physical restraints. During the 1820s and 1830s there was throughout the wider region from the southern Sudan to central Tanzania a prolonged drought.[3] Drier areas suffered terrible parching and famines which are recalled in traditions today. Under such conditions, moister areas such as central Buganda and southern Busoga might have experienced considerable food shortages. Several years of low rainfall in the region just north of Lake Victoria may have induced the Buganda court to mount large foraging campaigns to the east and may have also created conditions making such campaigns possible. Manpower would have been more available, movement of the army simpler, shelter less a problem. The freewheeling campaigns of Kakungulu, the Banyoro, and the Baganda around the normally well watered borderlands of the Buganda kingdom suggest a context of drought. The extent, severity, and duration of the Sewankambo campaign in Busoga also indicate exceptional conditions.

These are suggestions for which there is little explicit narrative support. But whatever the complex of permissive factors that shaped Sewankambo's campaign, it is clear that the conditions that had previously restricted Ganda armies to the southern and southwest parts of Busoga had changed. Sewankambo led his army across the Kiko without manifest difficulty and into the aggressive kingdom of Bugabula. There his army burned Naminage, Kagoda's capital. They captured and killed Wambuzi, Kagoda's only son (at the time). Kagoda himself fled north to a refuge near Kidera on the Lake Kyoga shore. There he remained for several years, exiled from the heartland of his kingdom. His plans for the expansion of the Bugabula state had been destroyed in a

matter of days. Eventually, several intermediaries traveled
to the capital of Buganda, and there they surrendered claims
to the lands west of the Nile and offered an enormous
amount of tribute to the Kabaka. Kabaka Kamanya in turn
gave notice of the ending of hostilities between his country
and Kagoda's. Kagoda returned and built a new palace at
Naminage, his domain reduced but not brought within the
regular administration of the Ganda state.[4]

With Naminage smoldering and Kagoda fleeing north,
the Ganda army moved east and attacked Luuka. It reached
Kiroba Hill and burned the capital of Wambuzi. Wambuzi,
receiving warning, fled to Nsambya where he hid among his
in-laws, of the Munhana clan, who were living just across
from Nafa's land. The Ganda army appears to have come
very close to attacking Nsambya, for as it reached the
Nabisira, it established a camp at Buyoga within several kilometers of Mukanni's shelter at Makutu and Wambuzi's
refuge at Nsambya.

Traditions suggest that the Ganda army, or a part of it,
camped at Buyoga for at least several months.[5] Raiding parties were sent on short foraging campaigns to the south and
to the north, collecting cattle, food, and women. Eventually, Sewankambo's army gave up Buyoga and moved
south along the western side of the Lumbuye. No crossing
of the Lumbuye was attempted; no large-scale foraging in
the Kigulu states to the east of the river was undertaken.
Rather, the army began a circuit back toward Buganda. It
passed the Luuka Hills and reentered the tributary states of
southwest Busoga and then crossed the Nile. Its long campaign east of the Nile was over and would be remembered
as a great success. The campaign was given the name
ekyetoloolo—"it went right around the whole country."

It was within this context of vigorous Ganda campaigning
along the northern frontier of Luuka that the small enclosure
of the young Mukama at Makutu was abandoned. Mukama,

his companions, and guardians left Makutu, presumably fleeing Ganda pressure. We learn next that the young Mukama—who must have been some seven to ten years old by the time the Baganda left Buyoga—had been installed in a new enclosure on the higher ground north of Nafa's community and north of Makutu. This new enclosure was circular in shape and some 120 meters in diameter, a substantial monument to the child's prestige. (See figure 3, chapter IV.) In scale, the enclosure rivaled the first palace of King Wambuzi at Kiroba Hill. The size of the enclosure suggests that even early in his life the young Mukama commanded a substantial following and, moreover, that the Ganda campaigns in Luuka did not disrupt this community of followers.

The *following* is a keystone of political life in the Lake Victoria region. The following transects the kinship-bounded homesteads and compounds in which children are raised and introduces new structures of relationships, joining individuals to nonkinship groups at one level and clients to patrons at another. Clients and followers lift the marginally known leader to higher levels of influence and prestige within the political world. Lowly followers with little wealth and no claims to title find new opportunities in the wake of their patron's elevation. The following is the vehicle for the mobilization of influence and the expression of prestige. It provides the patron with new possibilities for action and extends the range and diversifies the character of services to throne, court, and society. In Buganda, the following made possible the revolt of Semakokiro and then again the revolt of Kakungulu. The following brought Sewankambo from lowly status to the office of Ssekiboobo and helped him become the most important official in the government of Kabaka Kamanya. The following, promising mobility through recognition of achievement, brought tens of thousands of men into the campaign against the Busoga states. In Luuka, the following lifted Prince Wambuzi onto the royal stool upon the death of his father Inhensiko. And the following made it possible for Kalalu to achieve and maintain his influence as representative of the rulers of Luuka north of the Nabisira.

The principles of patronage and clientage, linked within the meaning of *following*, were played out thousands of times a day right around the Lake Victoria region, and these principles were expressed in manifold ways. The follower or client was prepared to exchange his courage or talent or loyalty for protection, recognition, cattle, land, a new life, access to upwardly mobile paths. For his part, the king or councilor or prince or priest had his own panoply of qualities that could draw people into his following and thereby enlarge his influence and enhance his prestige. Each had his own set of instruments that preserved and extended these qualities, binding individuals to him through land grants, appointments, service duties, and marriage. For the followers, there were varied levels and moments of risk, opportunity, and duty engrained in each patronage context.[6]

It would be an error to see these patronage and clientage relationships as enduring and concrete arrangements. Mobility upward and downward in both Buganda and Busoga states such as Luuka and Bugabula could be sharp and fast. More significantly, perhaps, the bond of fealty was loose. Both Buganda and Busoga were marked by high rates of geographical mobility in precolonial days. If a clientage arrangement proved to be unrewarding or slow to ripen in one place, the client would simply move elsewhere. The risks of political intrigue were high, and collaborators, provocateurs, and adventurers not only kept an eye open for opportunities to act but also watched for moments to escape. Opportunities for advancement within the political world of Luuka or Bugabula or Buganda typically meant levering opponents out of offices, land, service roles, and prestigious statuses. This engendered sharp and often bitter conflict in and around the court and ensured a constant flow of opportunists into and out of the political core of each state.

In respect to the following of the young Mukama, the particular framework of clientage and patronage was slightly different. First, the young Mukama's exceptional status placed him outside the normal political hierarchy. His prestige and importance, even influence, within wider Luuka society could grow or wane, but only within the context of the specific Mukama role. There would be no movement within the administrative hierarchy of Luuka, no opportunity for pulling clients to the highest level of offices in the Luuka state. Second, the young Mukama was, and would be, outside the sphere of day-to-day political competition. Mukama's sphere would be a place of political quiet within the Luuka world of knife-edged contention, jealousy, and intrigue. Some might be jealous of the young Mukama's following and of his weight within Luuka society, but no one could challenge or remove the young Mukama's divinely inspired sources of prestige. And third, because the intensity of political competition within and around Mukama's following would be dampened, the following itself came to be more stable in membership than any other following in precolonial Luuka. Families drawn within the community remained for several generations.

One may distinguish two points in the early years of the young Mukama's life when substantial numbers of new followers would have been drawn into his entourage. First, the news of the Mukama's birth brought to Makutu many men, women, and children. Young girls were given to the infant Mukama as wives. Ritual specialists came to assist in the ceremonies of his coming out and as advisors in the camp. Other individuals were attracted by the glitter of this new center of prestige, this new chance to rise above landlessness, danger, feud, and domestic trouble.

Second, it is clear that the Ganda campaign in Luuka, and
the humiliation of King Wambuzi, threw many people into
the young Mukama's following. During the occupation,
Wambuzi could not offer the protection that people expected
and required in order to meet basic needs. Lives were broken, families were torn apart to feed the Buganda segment
of the emerging nineteenth-century slave trade. Mothers
and daughters were seized for the courtiers of Buganda.
Homes were ruined and food carried off. It was a period of
upheaval and of flight. Many families fled north of the
Nabisira and sought safety and opportunities beyond what
had been the northern frontier of the Luuka state.

The young Mukama offered a form of leadership particularly suited to families in such crises and very different from
Wambuzi's, and yet the Mukama's authority was neither
revolutionary nor foreign. It fell within the framework of
Luuka polity and Luuka society. He was a member of the
royal family and the son of the ruler. Acknowledgment of
his authority would not constitute a decisive break with the
existing state, for there was no contradiction in recognizing
the king and serving the Mukama. On the other hand, his
divinely inspired authority drew on the original Mukama's
more earthly sources of prestige. These were symbolic in
one sense, but were more tangibly related to survivals of the
pastoral tradition: a mobility of leadership and a developing
sense of antipathy toward the realm of Buganda. Mukama's
presence was transitory, less visible, less focused, less open
to attack. The original Mukama was steadily on the move,
and similarly the young Mukama's qualities would not be
dissipated in flight. In contrast, the Luuka king could not
run and rule at the same time. Flight was disruptive of his
organized government. Flight made difficult the exaction of
tax to support the redistributive aspects of the economy.
Flight enhanced the contentious and countercentric ambitions of princes of the royal house. Flight and death inserted

gaps in the royal lineage, threatening disruption of the passage of authority and influence from father and son. The young Mukama was of the royal lineage, but in contrast to the other princes his unique basis of influence placed him apart from principles of succession and transfer of power, provided him with followers who joined him without a promise that their young patron might someday be a king. The young Mukama could ignite new relationships with desperate people in flight and infold them in a realm more of the mind than of territory.

It is both comprehensible and suggestive that few of the names of these earliest followers survive in the records of tradition. The traditions of association with a Mukama figure are considerably different from the traditions of association with kings and chiefs, which survive today in detail and in bulk. The traditions of association with the king survive in a relatively concrete form because the king provides offices, land, estates, and elevated status to his clients, and all of these have the potential of becoming hereditary. The children, the descendants, the beneficiaries of these early political associations preserve traditions of the court and of the grants as legal documentation of title. The Mukama, on the other hand, with feet in both this world and the other, is a more transient figure. The particular qualities that denote his special identity and describe his authority are not hereditary and thus survive only during his lifetime. The Mukama has few benefices to offer his early supporters that are material or that last into the generation of his followers' great-grandchildren. The Mukama is a momentary figure symbolically unsettled—in flight. The Mukama ideal is expressed in terms of steady movement onward from one enclosure to another, gathering new resources, meeting new challenges, but it is never expressed in terms of settling or putting down roots.

Moreover, the individual follower of the Mukama loses

his identity with lineage—cut off by his belief and service from the family in which he is born. Additionally, the Mukama attracts a high percentage of individuals without families, many infertile, old women and men, and this does not contribute to the formation of new generations of support from within his following, apart from his own children. Here again one glimpses a new community of the broken-network type. Family traditions are the threads with which one reconstructs in detail the membership of the following, and where men leave no children, their names and specific records of their pasts are likely to be forgotten and lost.

It is true that many followers of the first Mukama—the culture hero who crossed Busoga from east to west—are recalled. This was because his sons became "kings," and the early followers of Mukama and their children became the beneficiaries of political titles and rewards of hereditary character in the years of formation of the new northern states. In respect to a new Mukama of religious stature, where the Mukama's actions become political, hereditary benefices may be created that make the early followers more likely to endure in the record of tradition. As such benefices are most typically consolidated in marriages between the Mukama and the daughters and sisters among his followers, the traditions of marriage provide something of a record of the core of early supporters within the young Mukama's entourage.

The evidence on marriage suggests that in the early years of the young Mukama's life members of four clans constituted the core of his following. These were people of the Kisui clan, the Mususwa clan, the Maliga clan, and the Kaima clan. Members of these clans were living on the margins of the Luuka state in the years before the Ganda invasion. Some may have been involved with the Makutu camp. These early followers gave daughters to the young Mukama. It is of particular interest that a Mususwa group had been among the earlier companions of the first Mukama some five generations before the birth of Mukanni's child at Makutu, conveying from the past, perhaps, certain elements of the Mukama possession formula.

There was one additional individual the marriage records associate with the first years of the young Mukama's life. This is Naigedhe of the Kiyemba clan. Naigedhe appears to have played a particularly crucial role in the transfer of the young Mukama from the camp at Makutu to the new enclosure on the ridge. From the time of Inhensiko I, Naigedhe and his grandfather and his father and his children lived on the higher land of the ridge above the site of Nafa's community.[7] Their compound was closest to the site of the enclosure built for the new Mukama. Naigedhe was a grown man with several sons and daughters by the time the young Mukama's party crossed the Nabisira. He was, apparently, outside the realm of Nafa's authority and seems to have actively sought the transfer of the young Mukama to the north.

While the evidence of the early marriages provides the names of some—certainly only a core—of the people drawn into the early community centered on the young Mukama, there is evidence of quite different character on other early camp followers. The idea of the Mukama reaches back into the early period of Lwo activity in northern and eastern Busoga. Popular traditions today hold that it was among the enclosures of Lwo-speaking groups in eastern Busoga that the folk hero Mukama emerged before making his passage across Busoga. It was in the states of northern Busoga dominated by once Lwo-speaking people that the religious figures called *Bakama* (sing. *Mukama*) appeared. The Mukama idea embroidered the Bantu-speaking societies of northern and central Busoga with symbols and values associated with the earlier Lwo-speaking emigrants. The appearance of a Mukama figure in a sense revitalized the Lwo contribution within the world of northern Busoga.

85

There are a number of clans in Busoga today that apparently were once Lwo speaking. Some of these Lwo families achieved dominant political roles in new communities throughout northern Busoga. Others, however, did not achieve high office and moved across northern Busoga settling here and there, joining over a period of several generations the Bantu-speaking people among whom they settled.[8] By the close of the nineteenth century, there were some thirty clans in Busoga—of about 240 Soga clans—of apparent Lwo origin. Four once Lwo-speaking groups—of the Kiyaga, Musambwa, Mutiibwa, and Ndase clans—were settled on the ridge close to the site of the new enclosure built for the young Mukama, and presumably these groups composed part of the early following of Mukama, both on the ridge and still earlier at Makutu.

What is curious is that while these various clans of Lwo origin intermarry freely today, not a single group of Lwo origin was involved in a marriage with the young Mukama or, later, with his first sons. While persons of the Kisui, Mususwa, Maliga, Kaima, and Kiyemba clans were early supporters of the young Mukama and became linked to him through marriage, the once Lwo-speaking groups close by the new enclosure were in no instance connected through marriage. [9] Here, a strict marriage prohibition is disclosed. There is no explanatory or legal tradition or declaratory statement from an informant that tells us this, only the marriage evidence itself. But there is evidence from further afield that suggests such a situation was not unique to the Bunafu case; rather, this prohibition operated over a very large area, at least until the close of the nineteenth century. Not a single ruler in Bugabula, Buzaaya, or Luuka (all of them descended from once Lwo-speaking people) to the end of the nineteenth century was born of a mother of a clan of Lwo origin.[10] While prohibited from marriage with the new

Mukama, the Lwo families—with perhaps a strong disposition toward enclosure life—participated in the affairs of the young Mukama, won land and status without forming marriage ties to the Mukama, and very likely contributed to the preservation of Lwo values and ideas within the enclosure.

IV

Bukanga

YOUNG Mukama was a boy of some ten years when he was installed in the new enclosure north of the Nabisira. The new enclosure, erected on the grassy flat above Nafa's community, came to be called *Bukanga*, a name that recalled the important spear among the regalia of the infant Mukama at Makutu.[1] Bukanga was a large structure compared with royal and nonroyal compounds in the region of of Luuka. It was approximately 120 meters in diameter. (See figure 3.) It was the first of four enclosures built for Mukama Womunafu north of the Nabisira, and it was to be the birthplace of thirteen of the twenty-six sons of Mukama who survived to maturity (see table 1). Bukanga was to be occupied by Mukama himself for more than twenty years and by his wives and children and grandchildren for more than seventy.

For the descendant of Mukama, Bukanga represents a spatial context—a bounded residence at a particular and known site. It is the geographical locus of a catalogue of occurrences captured or indicated in tradition. Moreover, Bukanga is a period—one stage in the career of Mukama Womunafu and in the past of the Bunafu community, a period neatly enclosed by Mukama's installation there at the outset and, at the end, by his evacuation of the place.

While a "stage" is clearly evoked in these two respects, the record of tradition is in fact fragile. One *is* able to produce a simple catalogue of activities, incidents, and events that can be associated with the enclosure. But even in aggregate the explicit narratives of event tell us little. What is absent from tradition is a rendering of the Bukanga period

in the idiom and in the schema of the inheritors of that past.[2]
No tradition tells us that "this was a period of alliance and
maneuver," or that "Mukama Womunafu attempted in this
period to construct an alliance between old and new support," or that "this was a period of isolation and consolida-
tion," or that "Mukama employed several strategies to deal
with the close challenges of the Bugabula state and Nafa's
community."

What may be discerned of this period in general terms of
theme, program, and process comes from a network of inferences relating to the character of the site of the enclosure,
emerging from an analysis of affinal relationships centering
on Mukama, and drawing upon a consideration of the
design of the enclosure. These inferences are based upon
particularistic evidence (marriages, births, locations of residence, kinship data) rather than upon explanatory narratives. The inferences are based more upon observations of,
and reconstructions from, the remains of the Bukanga enclosure than upon narrative accounts of what the enclosure
was "really like." They are based upon more general
data—relating to the wider region and suggesting timing,
strategy, alliance, and conflict.

The Site

The collected traditions provide no reasons for the selection
of the particular site upon which Bukanga was erected, and
no such explicatory traditions should be expected. One cannot go directly into the minds of the people involved in the
selection of the site nor can one rely on retrospective expla-
nations in the oral testimonies. But a crude calculation of
the momentary advantages of the site for those whom we
understand to have been within the orbit of Mukama
Womunafu suggests that its selection was strongly influenced by the court of King Wambuzi of Luuka. While there

is always danger in attempting to read intent in effect and calculation in situation, the range of advantages of this particular site for the Luuka court does suggest that in the some ten years following the erection of the shelter at Makutu, King Wambuzi and his councilors had become well informed of conditions beyond the Nabisira and now sought to make the most of the potentially important challenge to kingly authority in the person of the young Mukama.

The site lay upon a grassy ridge, ideal for the keeping of the cattle that were so much a part of the effects of the Mukama figure. The site lay within 2,000 meters of the home of Mukanni's kin, thereby bringing the prince finally to the doorstep of his mother's people, fulfilling what seems to have been the earlier quest of his party. And the site lay within 800 meters of the compound of the queen mother of Luuka, the mother of King Wambuzi. (See map 11.) In the traditions of Luuka, Queen Mother Kabalu is accorded credit for the salvation of Luuka during the Ganda occupation. She is said to have protected the king and to have held together the families that had fled to the north. She is credited with having disciplined the ambitious brothers of King Wambuzi during a time when they might have forced their way to the throne through alliance with the Baganda. She is recalled as having restored Wambuzi to the throne and as having pressed the legitimacy of the lineage of Wambuzi after his death. As the mothers of the king, Kabalu's kin—of the Munhana clan—were the most trusted allies of Wambuzi.[3] The installation of the young Mukama close by and under the steady attention of such a group was a decision of superb acumen.

But this is not the only factor that may have induced Wambuzi and his councilors to favor the site. Standing above the hillslopes that run down to the Nabisira, the site isolated Nafa's community of refugees and restricted the expansion of Nafa's group up the ridge toward the north-

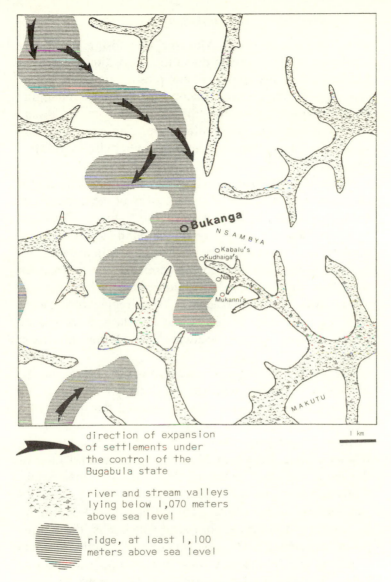

**direction of expansion
of settlements under
the control of the
Bugabula state**

**river and stream valleys
lying below 1,070 meters
above sea level**

**ridge, at least 1,100
meters above sea level**

MAP 11 • The Location of the Bukanga Enclosure. The Bukanga enclosure was sited on a grassy ridge on higher ground above, and just to the
north of, Nafa's compound. The site lay close to the lands of Mukanni's
kin and to the compound of the mother of King Wambuzi of Luuka. The
site also lay along the path of expansion of Bugabula settlements along
the ridge.

west. The site of young Mukama's enclosure stood as a challenge to Nafa's prestige and to his position outside the Luuka state. It juxtaposed a new prestigious figure whose sources of influence were incorporeal with an old figure of like character, providing the young Mukama an instant and local challenge of similar style. The new enclosure would draw new migrants who might otherwise join Nafa's community.

Moreover, the installation of the young prince on the ridge was a strong probe of the authority of the Luuka royal family north into the lands beyond the Nabisira. The flight of King Wambuzi and many Luuka families to the region north of the Nabisira and the ravages of war in the southern areas of Luuka had undoubtedly directed new interest toward this thinly occupied northern sphere. Within the following two or three decades, a large region beyond the Nabisira came fully within the Luuka state. Steadily, the Luuka capitals shifted northward behind this advancing front.[4]

There would be still further cause for Wambuzi and his advisors to be pleased with the site of the young Mukama's enclosure. The enclosure was so situated that it placed a man of the Luuka ruling family—a son of the ruler and a figure of unique magnetism—in the path of expansion of the Bugabula state. (See map 12.) Nadiope, the third ruler of Bugabula and the father of Wambuzi's contemporary Kagoda, had begun the process of expansion to the north and northeast of his capital. This expansion led eventually to conflict with the Bulamogi state which was, during this period, expanding to the west. In one of the battles between Bugabula and Bulamogi during this period, Nadiope was killed. Kagoda, Nadiope's son, took the throne and continued the program of expansion. As has been noted, it was Kagoda who extended his interests westward across the Nile, encouraging expansion through grants of land, es-

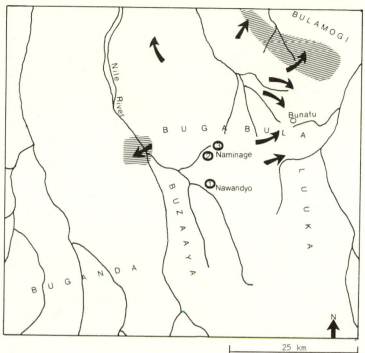

 approximate directions of expansion
of the Bugabula state during the reign
of Kagoda

areas of conflict along the fronts of
Bugabula expansion during Kagoda's time

○ early capitals of Bugabula

MAP 12 ● The Expansion of Bugabula during Kagoda's Reign. Kagoda was the fourth ruler of Bugabula and a contemporary of Wambuzi and Kakuku of Luuka and Kamanya and Suna of Buganda. His reign is recalled today as one of considerable expansion of the area under regular administration. Kagoda attempted to gain territory at the expense of his northeast neighbor Bulamogi (continuing a process of expansion begun there by his father Nadiope). Kagoda attempted to take control of areas under the tutelage of the Kabakas of Buganda on the western side of the Nile.He attempted to expand eastward into the regions to the north of the Kamirantumbu and Nabisira rivers along the Luuka frontier. Expansion along the Bulamogi and Buganda fronts led to serious military clashes with both states. By the close of Kagoda's reign, the expansion of the Bugabula state had been halted, even reversed, along all three fronts.

tates, and offices. It was Kagoda too who early in his reign encouraged the expansion of settlements eastward along the ridge, giving land to a family of the Mugwano clan and an estate to Munyirwa, a prince of the Bugabula ruling house. These lineages invited new settlers onto the eastern margins of the ridge, and together their influence was extended within two or three kilometers of the Nakaibaale stream by the time of the campaign of Sewankambo.[5]

Significantly, there was, as noted earlier, no geographical frontier between Nafa's lands and the lands of eastern Bugabula. The Nakaibaale stream and the Nabisira constituted a more formal and permanent boundary between the Luuka and the Bugabula kingdoms, but Wambuzi—in establishing his seventh son upon the ridge—placed this young and formidable challenge within an area more naturally a part of his neighbor Kagoda's domain and along the path of expansion of the Bugabula settlements. If the young Mukama's gathering continued to grow, the enclosure could become an effective node of resistence to Bugabula expansion and could strengthen the hand of the Luuka court in its program of expansion northward. If the young Mukama and his following were to present a challenge to the authority of the Luuka king, it would constitute no vital threat to the Luuka state, for the enclosure of the new Mukama was effectively isolated beyond the natural borders of Luuka. Indeed, if the young Mukama were to establish some sort of independent domain—as did two of his antecedent kin some fifty years before—it would at worst serve as a buffer between Luuka and its more aggressive neighbor to the west. These speculations, based upon considerations of strategic advantage and timing and naturally biased toward a perspective *of the Luuka court*, suppose a high degree of calculation at the court of Wambuzi and suggest that it was the court that was responsible for the selection of the site. Such speculation is not, of course, subject to proof. While the

94

quest for an authoritative answer to "why this particular site?" may be ultimately without success, the speculative approach, with stress on the potentials and on the effects, may bring us closer to comprehending the more essential significance of, if not the particular reasoning behind, the "decision."

THE DESIGN

The enclosure was built on fairly flat land in a grassy belt less than two kilometers north of the compound occupied by Nafa. Like the pastoral enclosures of his heroic antecedents (and like those enclosures of other pastoralists in the region), Bukanga was circular in shape. (See figure 3.) Its perimeter was marked by an interlacing ring of closely planted barkcloth, *mpano,* and *lukone* trees on the exterior side and by a woven fence on the interior. The Mukama's principal house was located at the center. Eventually, it was encircled by a number of smaller houses. Each of these was occupied by a wife and each was, like his own house, circular in shape with thatched roofing. The doorways of the wives' houses were aligned toward Mukama's house. The doorway of Mukama's house faced the main gate of the enclosure. One small gate opened to the west-northwest and was used by wives when going to their gardens outside the enclosure. The main gate was oriented to east-southeast and was used by visitors to enter and leave the enclosure.

The direction of alignment of the main gate of the enclosure may suggest certain perceptions of relatedness and subordination articulated among Mukama's coterie in the early phase of formation of this new community. The enclosure is, for the community around a Mukama, the tangible representation of the boundary between one world—that of Mukama—and the larger world from which these people came. In turn, the enclosure gate is the principal point of reference between the world within the enclosure and that

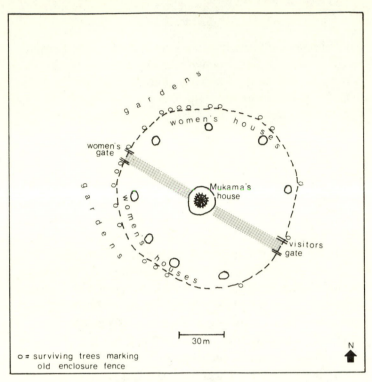

FIGURE 3 • Approximate Plan of the Bukanga Enclosure

world outside. The gate connects the affairs immediate to the enclosure to events and experience outside it through a network of paths and lines of communication that interlace courts, palaces, markets, and compounds. The ideas centering on Mukama challenge the world through the enclosure gate, and it is through the same gate that perceived challenges to Mukama will come. Where does the eye and where does the mind travel when perceiving the world through the orifice in the wall of the enclosure? To where does the well-worn path from the main gate lead? What message does the rendering of the gate and its relationship to principal pathways relay to nominal or pretentious superiors five, ten or twenty kilometers away? What signal does the gate alignment carry to intermediaries between court and enclosure and to migrants and refugees appearing before the big man of the enclosure? What connection is there between style and design and the conception of the place of the enclosure within the larger world of this region of Africa?

Generally in the precolonial period, the gates of important enclosures were aligned to reflect relationships of subordination and deference. Domains were not perceived in terms of concrete masses of land on a map but in terms of networks of deferential relationships, affirmed and routinized symbolically in language, posture, tribute, and architecture. The gate of an inferior official's enclosure was typically aligned toward the palace of his superior—that is, if the effect to be conveyed was one of deference. Alternatively, gates were occasionally oriented away from a nominal superior (perhaps toward some other figure of authority), a symbolic but active and visible "thumbing of the nose" at the pretentious superior's perceptions of domain and authority. Such architectonic insubordination undercut and retarded the formation of regular and deferential lines of communication between nominal inferior and pretentious superior and held the potential of contributing to the restructuring of "domain."

In the instance of the first enclosure of Mukama Womunafu, the gate opened to the east-southeast. The gate certainly did not direct the eye toward the palace of King Wambuzi nor did it orient toward the headquarters of Wambuzi's representatives in the north, the Muluuta lineage. Nor did it align toward any other node of authority in the immediate area. Rather, the orientation of the gate appears to have related Bukanga to the early enclosure of the heroic Mukama built on the eastern side of Busoga more than a century and a half earlier. (See figure 3 and inset, map 14,

97

chapter V.) The implication here is that the realm in which young Mukama was seen to operate by those followers who constructed his first enclosure was more the incorporeal world of the spirit of the heroic Mukama who crossed Busoga from east to west and less the earthly world of King Wambuzi who was, in these years, attempting to reconstruct his kingdom in the wake of the devastating *ekyetoloolo* campaign.

THE NANGWE ALLIANCE

At a more explicit level, the evidence of tradition reveals a network of relationships formed in the early occupation of Bukanga between Mukama Womunafu and one kin group living within the area of Nafa's authority on the slope of the ridge. We learn that Mukama Womunafu introduced his sister Napiri, who had been living in the palace of Wambuzi before the *ekyetoloolo* sacking, to Kudhaiga, a man of the Nangwe clan. In the Lake Victoria region—indeed, over much of Africa—marriages are perceived as accessible and vital mechanisms for engaging support, for enlarging and strengthening the social network within which one lives and works. These linkages among in-laws (*bako, bakoddomi, bakoirume*) are called *buko* ties. Given the play of duties and responsibilities among *buko* relations—how people believe they should behave toward their in-laws—every marriage is strategic both in its formation and its function. The marriage in part gives shape to the status, mobility, and power of both the lineage of the wife and the lineage of the husband. Each marriage locks together new segments of kinship groups into a broader network of interdependent relationships. This network enlarges and refines the support one can call upon in time of need or crisis, which one makes use of in everyday activities as well, and through which one defines his own identity and ambitions. The *buko* relation-

98

ship is a contractual bond between social groups. It is a bond that is, relative to other social ties, long enduring. While clientage ties may be quickly and sharply broken, while friendship ties may fall away as the consequence of high rates of geographical mobility, the deeper relations established through *buko* may survive the marriage itself in the networks of relations and in the obligations placed upon both the children of a marriage and the lineages of the immediate parties. Because the marriage is a great statement which emits signals relating to status and ambition and because the *buko* relationship has the capacity to operate over distances and over time, the marriage is approached with an interest, a strategic sense, a knowing of circumstance, unparalleled in any other field of social and political activity.

Near the crest of the ridge, Kudhaiga took Napiri as a wife and thereby established a relationship of importance between his lineage and the young Mukama and his encampment. Within a few years, Kudhaiga's brother's son Mutankwa gave to Mukama Womunafu two girls: Basuwaba and Mudondo. This intensified the *buko* relationship between these two groups. (See figure 4.) The two women given by Mutankwa were to gain preeminent roles within the Bukanga enclosure. They were the mothers of Womunafu's first two sons, the mothers of several daughters, the mothers of six of the first twenty children who survived to maturity.

That at this moment and at this place Kudhaiga's and Mutankwa's segments of the Nangwe clan should establish such an important role within the enclosure and within the following of Womunafu is significant. The advisors within Womunafu's camp had not failed to note the position of the Nangwe groups in the area north of the Nabisira. Just several hundred meters to the southwest of Bukanga—directly across the Nakaibaale from King Wambuzi's mother's compound—lay Kudhaiga's lands. (See map 11.) Kudhaiga's household, though within the circle of Nafa's authority, was established upon the most northerly lands with Nafa's world—closest to the crest of the ridge and to the new enclosure. If Mukama Womunafu were to make inroads into Nafa's community and to strengthen thereby his own grip on the area, Kudhaiga's people, close neighbors, would have appeared as the first target.

Of more strategic importance to the Luuka kingdom generally was the position of the Nangwe settlers throughout this region to the north of the Nabisira. Just to the west of Bukanga lay several of the outposts of Bugabula's expansion to the east. This was Kagoda's Bugabula, and great numbers of Nangwe men were arriving at Kagoda's court from northeast Busoga during this time. The Nangwe clansmen were happy beneficiaries of offices and estates in Bugabula right through Kagoda's reign.[6] Nangwe settlements along the eastern frontiers of Bugabula were potential nodes of sympathy and alliance in Kagoda's time and would undoubtedly have been viewed by Luuka's leaders as loci of ambivalence, if not resistance, requiring strong action. The installation of Mukama Womunafu directly between the

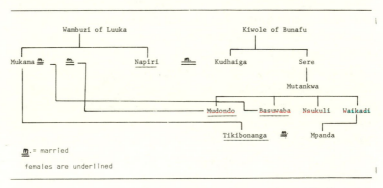

FIGURE 4 ● The *Buko* Network: Mukama Womunafu and Kudhaiga's Lineage

Nangwe settlements along the Nakaibaale and the expanding Bugabula state was—whether done consciously or accidentally—an action that would retard the formation of alliances between Nangwe settlements and Bugabula in this open region. The relationships established between Womunafu and Kudhaiga clearly were not accidents and would have effectively defused such predispositions toward alliance with Bugabula. At the same time, these new relationships would have cut into Nafa's coterie of supporters.

NEW SUPPORTERS AND OLD FRIENDS

Looking at the provenance of the thirteen sons born at Bukanga who survived to maturity, one may perceive three categories into which these data fall. First, six of the sons (including the three sons of Nangwe mothers mentioned above) were born to women from lineages living within the purview of Nafa: two women from the Nangwe lineage, one woman from the Mabandha lineage, and one from the Kabambwe lineage. Second, three sons were born to women associated with the Makutu camp: one woman from the Kaima clan, one woman from the Maliga clan, and one woman from the Mususwa clan. Third, four sons were born to women whose families came from the close vicinity of the Bukanga enclosure but not from within Nafa's domain: one woman from the Kiyemba clan (one lineage of which appears to have played a role in the transfer of Mukama from Makutu to Bukanga), one woman from the Kisui clan, a lineage of which was established about two kilometers south-southwest of Bukanga, and one woman from the Kadhubuli clan, a segment of which arrived at Bukanga some time after the Bukanga enclosure was completed.

What is suggested here is that in these crucial marriage arrangements Mukama Womunafu and his close advisors struck balances among several considerations: the rein-

101

TABLE 1

PROVENANCE OF THE THIRTEEN SONS (SURVIVING TO
MATURITY) OF MUKAMA WOMUNAFU BORN AT BUKANGA

Sequence of Birth	Name of Son	Mother's Clan	Point of Association
1	Inhensiko	Nangwe	Nafa's
2	Galya	Nangwe	Nafa's
3	Kyaliwumba	Kaima	Makutu
4	Nhiro	Maliga	Makutu
5	Lwaidho	Kiyemba	Bukanga vicinity
6	Ibanda	Kisui	Bukanga vicinity
7	Wambuzi Kabodi	Mususwa	Makutu
8	Ibanda Wamugo	Mabandha	Nafa's
9	Kinooge	Mabandha	Nafa's
10	Togolo	Kisui	Bukanga vicinity
11	Mufuta Naita	Nangwe	Nafa's
12	Kaisemutala	Kadhubuli	Bukanga vicinity
13	Ndhaye	Kabambwe	Nafa's

forcement of ties with the older core of support from
Makutu (which one may suppose was positive and emotional), the structuring of new support within the neighborhood of the enclosure (the interest in which was tacti-
cal), and the effect of the close presence of Nafa's community (the interest in which was strategic). One set of Womunafu's marriages emphasized security for the refugees who
had come into Mukama's fold during the time of
ekyetoloolo. A second category of marriages may be seen to
have emphasized security for the camp of Mukama as a
whole within the vicinity of the Bukanga enclosure. A third
category of marriages may be seen to have undermined Nafa's prestige, applying pressure to kin groups once under
Nafa's domination. (See table 1.)

What is also remarkable about the inventories of marriages and marriage alliances at Bukanga is what is not there. First, apart from the link with the Kadhubuli family, no *new* relationships through marriage are noted *following* the erection of the enclosure. While the Makutu years may be seen as ones in which refuge was the fundamental impetus giving form to Mukama's community in its period of emergence, refuge appears to have become much less important in the elaboration of relationships at Bukanga. Here, the creation and reinforcement of ties with groups already established in the immediate area seem crucial. Second, no marriages reveal links between Mukama Womunafu (or members of his following) and any of the commoner lineages then prominent within the Luuka state. Third, no *buko* relationship was created with the Muluuta representatives of the Luuka kings in the north until the last decades of the century.

What is suggested then by this analysis of the marriage inventories is that the *buko* relationship, which is the accessible point of observation of the networks of relationships that composed the small community around Womunafu, operated as both an integrative and a segregative device. It created within and around the Bukanga enclosure not only a network of relationships centered on the Mukama figure, but also a network oriented both to the early experience of refuge and to the immediate circumstances of neighborhood: the close front of expansion on the part of the Bugabula kingdom and the contiguity of Nafa's community. But it also—in its segregative aspect—contributed to a community apart from the wider world. In the marriage records no indications survive of any attempt on the part of Mukama Womunafu to create or to reestablish links beyond the immediate world before him. In terms of networks of *buko* relationships, one may characterize the Bukanga period as one of insulation, if not isolation.

This is not surprising. The enclosed world of a Mukama

is quintessentially isolated. The Mukama's residence is built outside the realm of conventional life and exists as something visibly unique and enclosed. Long-distance linkages with other centers of power or prestige are unnecessary. Associations with courts and officials near or far are neither required nor sought. The community of Mukama was a community unto itself, ideologically self-sufficient, this separation from the world all the more remarkable given the thickly knit network of contacts and relations that constituted the regional economy.

The grand enclosure built for Mukama on the ridge signaled both separation and importance. It conformed to a pastoral design in a region only marginally pastoral. Its gate opened the life of the enclosure not to a world of demand, tribute, and political adventure but rather to a realm that joined the living and possessed Mukama with the dead, bringing the ancient heroes within the existing world. The size of the enclosure reflected the considerable labor and service that Mukama could draw from the vicinity of Bukanga. Women gave varieties of service at the enclosure and in their demeanor enshrined the concept of *service* to Mukama. The very name Womunafu, which Mukama was given at Bukanga, celebrates the importance of female service in the enclosure, the importance of women to the maintenance of a heroic figure such as Mukama.[7]

To say that this community at Bukanga was effectively detached from the world of Luuka is not to suggest that there were no cleavages in role or status within Mukama's community. In particular, Mukama was lifted away from the people around him. As an infant Mukama was nurtured with this distinctive role. He was kept in his house of birth both actually and symbolically much longer than other infants of his day. He was surrounded by servants not his kin and was raised away from the lineage folk of both his mother and his father. As a young man he was surrounded by women and through them linked to a large number of *bako*. He was trained in the language and skills of the *balaguzi*, and to him came the sick, weak, and frightened for help. He was given lavish gifts by visitors from outside his community and by those within. Songs were sung to him, and drums were beaten in his honor. He was praised often at Bukanga in the *kugongereza* style. This was a form of chant typically reserved for rulers. The praise was sung by two men who went on and on until they fell from exhaustion. There is a praise text recorded in 1971 that may be similar to the praises of the Bukanga period.

> Womunafu, the owner, the owner, the owner. He is brown. He is light. He is tall. He is fat. His father the Goat. His mother the Namunhole. His mother the Namunhole is no longer a Munhole. His mother Naigobe. Womunafu Ikanga. Mukama. Mukama is brown. He is light. Mukama is tall. The Namunhole is no longer a Munhole. He is the owner. The owner. Mukama shall supply. The throat is blocked. It wants beer. Mukama Womunafu. Mukama Namutukula. Mukama is tall. He is stout. His body is light. His wives bring their food. If you bring a small amount, stay away. Mukama. Mukama Womunafu.[8]

Such praise together with a complex of deferential language and manners wove a barrier that set off Womunafu, the possessed one, the Mukama, from the people around him at Bukanga. This was Bukanga in 1850, a small world surely understood by its inhabitants to be both separate and different from the worlds around it.

V

Kyonzira

AT mid-century, the royal enclosures of Luuka remained far from Bukanga. It was a time of relative calm. Upon Wambuzi's death (ca. 1841), a son, Kakuku, succeeded to the kingship against little opposition. The interests of Buganda were shifting away from major campaigns of plunder in Kyaggwe and Busoga, though this was rather more a case of work completed than plan deferred. Buganda's strategic momentum was now directed toward the southwest, toward Buddu and beyond—down the trade routes of the western grasslands which linked with the growing trade between the Indian Ocean metropoles and the East African interior.

For the people of Bukanga, the problems of the world were *not* close at hand. The trade goods of the East African long-distance routes would not reach Bukanga for another thirty years. It would be some forty years before someone from the region north of the Nabisira would travel as far as the Buddu region of western Buganda and return. But what was close and certain was that the horizon of the Bugabula state lay only several thousand meters to the west. And the small and challenging domain of Nafa was much closer. The absence of intense and violent civil conflict within Luuka and within neighboring states meant that few refugees joined the Bukanga community during these quiet years following Kakuku's accession. Mukama Womunafu's support was becoming old. His sons were approaching maturity. The ideal of the heroic figure of Mukama on the move—frequently revivified by new followers—was giving

106

way to the more mundane interests of the settled leader of a new community.

But between about 1855 and 1860, this picture of calm is displaced by one of upheaval. The period of troubles for Luuka began, popular tradition records, with the tasting of dried bananas *(mutere)* in the royal enclosure of Buganda. The food was a "gift of tribute" from Kakuku, ruler of Luuka, to the Kabaka of Buganda. This weighty token, carried to Buganda by hundreds of men, was found to contain human feces, so the story goes. It was no small insult. Kakuku and several of his important chiefs were executed in Buganda.[1]

When the news of Kakuku's death reached Luuka, Kabalu, the mother of Wambuzi, sought to place Kakuku's son Mudhungu on the throne. But Mudhungu was still young and could not be quickly brought to the capital. Mudhungu was living at Naminage, one of the palaces of Kitamirike I, Gabula Namugweri, ruler of Bugabula. While many of those who would have supported Kabalu and Mudhungu were either caught in Buganda or dead, the supporters of a brother of Kakuku, Kalogo, quickly arrived at the Luuka capital in strength. Kalogo was installed, and Mudhungu returned to Bugabula, this time in hiding. The death of Kakuku and the accession of Kalogo opened a wild period of contention among various parties in Luuka. Kalogo would survive on the throne for only a year or so, and within the period from approximately 1855 to 1859, four princes would sit on the throne of Luuka. Ganda adventure and intrigue grew, fueling the conflicts that swirled around the court. Hundreds of refugees fled the Luuka center and the strongholds of the competing princes. These refugees began arriving in numbers north of the Nabisira, and more than a few arrived at Bukanga. By 1860, a new enclosure—*Twesudde*—had been built for Mukama

Womunafu at a site some thousand meters south of Bukanga (see map 13). The transfer of Mukama to Twesudde inaugurated a new period in the history of Bunafu.

Mukama Womunafu had occupied the Bukanga enclosure for nearly a quarter of a century. Superficially, this ex-

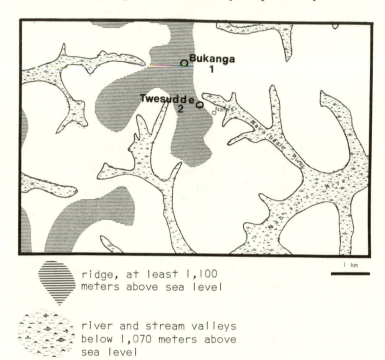

≋ ridge, at least 1,100
   meters above sea level

river and stream valleys
below 1,070 meters above
sea level

O   sites of enclosures of Mukama

Map 13 ● The location of Twesudde Enclosure. The execution of Kakuku in Buganda opened a wild "era of princes" in Luuka. Many groups fled the conflicts that swirled around the courts of Luuka in the years following Kakuku's death. Kalogo ruled Luuka for only a year or so, and then his brother Kibalya succeeded. Other princes sought to build strongholds of support, and several rallied Ganda support for their claims to the throne. Luuka seethed with tension. In the early years of this era of princes—probably between 1855 and 1860—Mukama Womunafu left his Bukanga enclosure and settled in a newly built enclosure which came to be called "Twesudde."

108

ceptionally long occupation suggests a high degree of emotional, perhaps spiritual, attachment to the Bukanga site. But Mukama is a figure quintessentially mobile, and the maintenance of residence for such a long period suggests more fundamental constraints on his movements. A brief story attributed by one informant to a woman long deceased provides a glimpse of such constraint.

> A very old woman, Tikibonanga at Nsambya, had this story to tell about Mukama. Mukama came from the Bukooli side and reached Naibiri and built a capital called Naibiri. The gate of the enclosure was called Kazigo. He then went from Naibiri to Nsambya near Bunafu. Here he had a *kyonzira* and he stayed for some time. From Nsambya, Luuka, he went to Kebagani where he divided the land among his children. Then he went to Bunyolo.[2]

At the time of recording this text in December 1966, and indeed until late 1971, this story appeared to the author to offer just one more variant of the popular tradition concerning the passage of the heroic Mukama from the eastern side of Busoga to the west. The reference to the enclosure built at Naibiri conformed to an array of evidence from other texts. However, there was in the recorded traditions no further reference to, or evidence relating to, this allegation that an enclosure had been built for the heroic Mukama figure in the area of Nsambya.

It was not until late 1971 that it was noted that Nsambya lay just 300 meters across the Nakaibaale stream from the first enclosure of the nineteenth-century Mukama figure, Mukama Womunafu. Here was an explanation for the reference to the enclosure at Nsambya. The December 1966 text simply joined together two stories that were distinct but related: the one story of Mukama's passage across Busoga and the second story of the emergence of a latter-day and quite local Mukama figure.

Attention was also drawn to the *kyonzira* element which did not appear in other variants of the general Mukama tradition and which could be a critical component of a local Mukama tradition centered on Womunafu of Bunafu. A *kyonzira* is a cursed amulet. Hung over a door or placed on a path, it will halt the passage of those disposed to acknowledge its force. It is invested with this force by a specialist *(mufumu)* on behalf of someone who fears the actions of another person or persons. Control of the charm strengthens the confidence of the party for whom it is made and sends piercing and frightening signals to those who might fear it is intended for them. It has the power to kill. Today, the *kyonzira* is sought most commonly by individuals who feel threatened in situations of competition: getting jobs, at the workplace, school examinations, marital troubles, and land disputes. The *mufumu* advises his client on the handling and placement of the amulet. Specialists are also sought by those requiring protection from the *kyonzira*.

The brief text relating the story of Mukama and the *kyonzira* reports that the amulet was found at "Nsambya near Bunafu" and that it brought Mukama's journey to a halt. At first examination, the text appeared to suggest that the charm in question—or the forces or conditions it symbolized—were found as Mukama's party was heading in a westward direction. The implication was that the *kyonzira* was met just to the *west* of the site where Mukama halted.

As more was learned by the author about Bunafu and the locations of enclosures in the vicinity of "Nsambya near Bunafu" where a Mukama—Mukama Womunafu—did indeed stay, attention shifted from the west to the *south*, to the expanse of ridge and slope between the first and second enclosure occupied by Womunafu. Mukama Womunafu had four enclosures, occupied serially. In each instance of relocation, residence shifted southward. While the heroic Mukama of more general Soga tradition may have traveled in a predominantly westward direction, Mukama Womunafu over his long lifetime moved southward, down the ridge toward the Nabisira. (See map 14.) If *his* passage were halted temporarily by a *kyonzira*—or by forces represented in the story by a charm—then the cursed amulet (or forces) would have been located to the south of one of his enclosures.

While there is unfortunately no explicit narrative that neatly settles this question for us, there are several pieces of evidence that when viewed together would seem to clarify the problem considerably. Just 400 meters south of the site of the first enclosure of the young Mukama at Bukanga there is a small pool called "Nakyere." Today the word has no meaning for the people living close by. It is just the name of the pool and is supposed to have "always been the name." But what was not known by the people of Bunafu in 1972 when the research on Bunafu's past was being completed was that in northeast Busoga and in Lwo-speaking Budama County to the east of Busoga and in the Lwo-speaking areas of northern Uganda, the *Nakyere (Na-kyeri or Na-kyere;* or *Acher, Achiel)* is a sacred object of great power. Sometimes it takes the form of a drum, a harp, or an amulet. In Bukono, Bulamogi, and Busiki in northeast Busoga, an area upon which Lwo-speaking people made a striking impact, the most important royal instruments are called *binakyeri (bi-nakyeri, bina-achiel).* (See map 15.)

At the core of this area of northeast Busoga lived the ancestors of Nafa of Bunafu: the Baganza. Traditions record that the Baganza played an important role as ritual specialists in the courts of Bukono. The Baganza would have been familiar with the *Nakyere* or *Achiel* objects. These objects were the preeminent legitimizing symbols of the dominant families of the area including the royal house of Bukono.[3] The Baganza would have been aware of the sacredness of these names and objects to Lwo-speaking and once Lwo-speaking peoples of the area.

Traditions indicate that Nafa's antecedents came from the

111

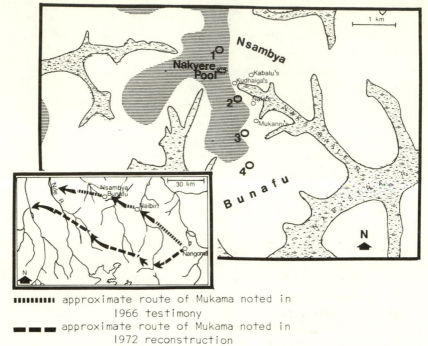

 approximate route of Mukama noted in
        1966 testimony
■ ■ ■ approximate route of Mukama noted in
        1972 reconstruction
◯ Mukama's enclosures at Bunafu
river and stream valleys
below 1,070 meters above
sea level

 ridge, at least 1,100
meters above sea level

MAP 14 • Mukama's Passage: An Interruption. An oral testimony recorded in 1966 relates that "Mukama," while crossing Busoga from east
to west, "had a *kyonzira* (at Nsambya near Bunafu) and he stayed there
for some time." The route said to have been followed by Mukama across
Busoga in this text does not conform to the route of the heroic Mukama as
reconstructed by the present writer. But within the immediate area of
Nsambya and Bunafu there was clearly a "progress" of Mukama. This
was the southward movement of the residences of Mukama through the
construction of four enclosures on and below the ridge north of the Nabisira. Lying between the sites of the first two enclosures—Bukanga and
Twesudde—is the Nakyere Pool which could represent the *kyonzira*
noted in the 1966 testimony. The inset presents a small map of the general region of Busoga showing the route of Mukama alleged in the 1966
testimony, which noted the *kyonzira*, and the reconstructed route of the
heroic Mukama presented by the author in a 1972 publication.

112

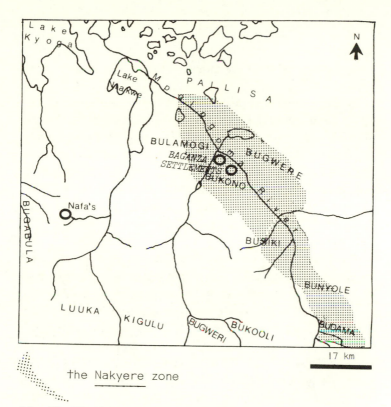

the Nakyere zone

MAP 15 ● The Nakyere Zone of Northeast Busoga. The *Nakyere* is a sacred object of great power in northeast Busoga and in adjacent areas to the east of the Mpologoma River. It is a royal emblem and may take the form of a drum, a harp, or an amulet. It is the *Achiel* of Lwo-speaking peoples, and the groups assuming dominant positions along the Mpologoma River were once Lwo speaking. The map denotes the general region within which are located the earliest capitals of Bukono, Busiki, and Bulamogi. And it was within this zone in Bukono that the Bakalimo/Baganza settled, and it was from among these Bakalimo/Baganza that the lineage of Nafa emerged.

courts of Bukono. Traditions identify Nafa as the one person in the Bunafu area who controlled knowledge of the use of charms and amulets.[4] The implication is that Nafa not only had the skills to give frightening force to a physical object, but that he also would have understood which symbols would have the strongest impact on a collection of people who surrounded themselves with objects and ideas of Lwo cast.

What is suggestive about the Nakyere pool, beyond carrying the name of the most important of such ritual objects, is that it is located along the path between what was the core of Nafa's community and the site of the Bukanga enclosure. It could also have been taken as the most prominent physical feature distinguishing the more open land of the ridge around Bukanga from the land that begins to fall toward the Nakaibaale and the Nabisira and that was occupied by Nafa's community

Moreover, Nafa was not only the one figure in the area with the skills and knowledge to invest an amulet with such force, he also had the strongest interest in preventing the expansion of Mukama's party into the area in which Nafa perceived himself as dominant. Nafa had a strong interest in establishing a clear boundary between the land and people under his control and the activities up on the ridge. More particularly, a boundary at Nakyere would have maintained Kudhaiga's family of the Nangwe clan within the purview of Nafa's authority. Kudhaiga's people lived just south of Nakyere on the most northerly lands under Nafa's control, and Mukama was in this period cultivating relations with them. That Nafa might have attempted to limit such relationships through the creation of a barrier between Bukanga and Kudhaiga could only be expected in the situation. The employment of powerful instruments to do so instantly and dramatically would have been a natural response to such a challenge from the higher lands of the ridge.

Even more, Nafa would have sought to hinder any attempt by Mukama Womunafu and his supporters to erect an enclosure on the margins of the ridge to the south of Bukanga and Nakyere. Such a site would have clearly placed Mukama in a position from which he could actively

114

settle the lands of the hillslope with his own supporters and thereby direct an immediate challenge at Nafa's control of the land and of the population living upon it.

The *kyonzira* text expresses delay. Mukama was delayed by a charm across his path. The reconstruction of Mukama's career indicates that Mukama stayed at Bukanga for an exceptionally long time, very likely to the peril of the ideal of the Mukama "on the move." What is interesting, perhaps revealing, here, is that the name of the second enclosure was "Twesudde"—"we have kept distance," "we have kept ourselves removed," "we have stood apart," "we have been held back."

This long exegesis of this brief text is largely suppositional. There is no way to prove that a *kyonzira* was physically cast upon the waters or upon the path of Mukama Womunafu and his party in the mid-nineteenth century. No source has provided an explicit narrative that proclaims this happened, and no other evidence is available that would raise the levels of confidence in the selection and deployment of the quite scattered data used in the reconstruction offered above. What we know for certain, however, is that a second enclosure was erected to the south of the Nakyere pool between approximately 1855 and 1860, that, after nearly a quarter of a century at Bukanga, Mukama evacuated that enclosure, leaving behind most of his wives and most of his children. The particular timing of this transfer of residence suggests that Mukama Womunafu was responding to several important new conditions.

New Refugees

This was a period marked by intense civil conflict in Luuka. As noted, four rulers sat on the throne during the short space of four years. Two of them had been murdered and a third chased from the country. New refugees appeared north of the Nabisira. These refugees, like those who fled the *ekye-toloolo* campaign some twenty years earlier, would have been attracted to this node of prestige and protection. Here was a Luuka prince of great attractiveness outside the active political life of Luuka and, unlike many of his collateral siblings, without pretensions to the throne. His enclosure was a sacred retreat, a place of safety in a wider region of insecurity and reprisal.

For those refugees still girded for political adventure within Luuka, Mukama's place lay just across the Nakai-baale stream from the compound of the family of Kabalu, once queen mother and the most powerful figure of the eras of Wambuzi and Kakuku.[5] (See map 5 in chapter I and map 13.) It would be Kabalu's family that over the next few years would lead a campaign to still Ganda adventure and intrigue through mediation and gift. Kabalu's kin and allies would, as a final act in 1870, bring stability to Luuka through seating Wambuzi's grandson Mudhungu Kalimwigi on the throne. In doing so, they reestablished the principle of filial succession, thereby ensuring the ultimate succession of Nabwana Inhensiko II (Mudhungu's eldest son) and silencing at least momentarily the contentious claims of younger princes.[6]

Traditions also relate that the northern reaches of Luuka were becoming more attractive for settlement. The Muluuta group was becoming increasingly important north of the Nabisira. Commoners, they remained the "much loved representatives of the Luuka kings in that area." The virulence of Ganda campaigning and raiding in the south near the old capitals of Luuka and the consequent and progressive reforestation of parts of the south, which extended the range of the biting *mbwa* fly, contributed to the general shift of population northward.[7]

The refugees who reached the Bukanga area in this period constituted a second generation of newcomers. Among the refugees there were a number of women. Their arrival at Bukanga brought them into potential relationship with Mukama Womunafu. The new men included Mpiti of the Nkwanga clan, Lukuya of the Luuka royal house, Bahano of the Muvu clan, Isabirye of the Mukubembe clan, and Mpata of the Kidhuggu clan.[8] They offered to Mukama Womunafu a new network of supportive relationships. Their appearance north of the Nabisira made possible a reinvigoration of some of the old ideals of leadership, association, and movement that gave birth to the first community focused on the infant Mukama at the Makutu camp.

Lloyd Fallers, in discussing twentieth-century communities in Busoga, argued that for a chief to sustain his capacity to rule, he must resolve the conflict between his role as leader of his own family and his role as leader of a community that extends beyond his family.[9] Successful authorities must complement, balance, or even counteract the influence and pressure of close people and relatives around them. The redefinition of relations between chief and kin is accomplished through the establishment of links outside the circle of kin. New ties—through the institutions of marriages and clientship—are created with groups from outside the old networks. In this, the attraction and integration of new settlers is an important component of this struggle to escape the constraining bonds of kinship. While Fallers' argument turned on this kinship nexus, an equally fundamental distinction may have operated in terms of *old* as against *new* support, whether kin or not.

Was a desire to move out among new people at the heart of the apparently regenerative transposition of Mukama Womunafu to a new enclosure? The record of marriages that tradition provides suggests so. Only one of the marriages in the second enclosure linked Womanafu with a family involved with the first enclosure at Bukanga. (See table 2.) Mukama's first wives at Bukanga were by this time old,

117

Kyonzira

TABLE 2

PROVENANCE OF THE NINE SONS (SURVIVING TO MATURITY)
OF MUKAMA WOMUNAFU BORN AT TWESUDDE

Sequence of Birth	Name of Son	Mother's Clan	Point of Association	Mother
14	Isumwa	Mukubembe	New immigrant	Nabirye
15	Kimwena	Mukubembe	New immigrant	Nabirye
16	Kiwunha	Kiyemba	Bukanga vicinity	Taidhikwiza
17	E. Walugundha	Kisikwe	New immigrant	Kahala
18	Wambuzi Kimbibi	Makiika	New immigrant	Zimba
19	Minka Kayaga	Kiyemba	Bukanga vicinity	Taidhikwiza
20	W. Kidhuggu	Kidhuggu	New immigrant	Kyeyuha
21	Z. Wambuzi	Mukubembe	New immigrant	Kivunani
22	Inhe. K. Mpata	Kidhuggu	New immigrant	Kawala

the greying daughters of quite ancient supporters firmly established in the community in their own right. The evidence reveals a substantial break between Bukanga and Twesudde. Twesudde itself stands as a small new world where Mukama could weave a new network of support from groups only just then arriving north of Nabisira.

The new support at Twesudde was not in any way minimal. The Twesudde site was heavily forested. The clearance of the site and erection of the enclosure imply not merely the availability of considerable labor but represent the reassertion of Mukama Womunafu's rights to exploit more than just some maintenance services. A massive rendering of labor was required to erect such a substantial enclosure on a forested site. It was, in fact, the largest project ever undertaken on Mukama's behalf. The new site also presented to Mukama Womunafu the opportunity to settle his new people on adjacent lands. Moreover, the new site provided Mukama's women with good and close gardens, while the former palace by this time would have certainly provided little room for maneuver.

118

OLD SONS

While new people such as Mpiti, Mpata, and Bahano posed the potential for regeneration of the community at a new enclosure, the achievements at Bukanga made a shift of residence possible. By 1860, several of Mukama's sons were mature and ready, likely eager, to assume responsibilities in the growing community centered on Bukanga. As a young boy, Mukama was surrounded by women, and we can be certain that Mukama was still very young when these women started bearing his children. An analysis of names suggests that Mukama Womunafu had at least six sons by the time of King Wambuzi's death.[10] There was Galya, whose mother was Basuwaba, a Nangwe girl. There was Kyaliwumba, the son of Mukanni, the Kaima girl. There was Nhiro, whose mother was of the Maliga clan and who was raised near the Mukutu camp. There was Lwaidho, son of Nzirawengwa, daughter of Naighedhe of the Kiyemba clan whose home was very close to Bukanga. And there was Ibanda, son of Kwebwika. Kwebwika was a girl of the Kisui clan. Her father had land four kilometers south of Bukanga—just north of the Nabisira.

By 1860, Mukama Womunafu had made several decisions in respect to these young men. Ibanda was granted land very near the home of his mother's people, the Kisui, lands that ultimately would be designated Bubanda *kisoko*. Nhiro was given a grant close to the old Makutu camp and went to live there among his mother's people, the Maliga. Galya was given an estate just southwest of Nafa's area, close to the compound of his mother's people of the Nangwe clan: one segment of Kudhaiga's lineage. And Lwaidho was entrusted with the most important grant, the old enclosure at Bukanga. Bukanga lay close to the homes of his mother's people—Naigedhe's lineage of the Kiyemba clan. (See map 16.)

These were important grants, immediately strengthening

119

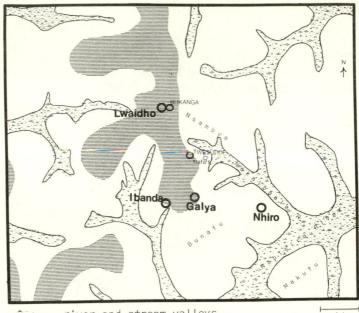

 river and stream valleys
below 1,070 meters above
sea level

ridge, at least 1,100
meters above sea level

⭕ Mukama's enclosures (1&2)

 locations of four sons'
enclosures

MAP 16 ● Mukama Womunafu's Oldest Sons. By about 1860, at least
four of Mukama Womunafu's sons born at Bukanga were old enough to
be given important responsibilities. Mukama granted land and privileges
to Galya, Ibanda, Lwaidho, and Nhiro. Each was established close to his
mother's kin on or below the ridge. Ibanda, Galya, and Nhiro built enclosures some 2,000 meters south of Bukanga, and Lwaidho was left with
the Bukanga enclosure when Mukama moved to his new enclosure at
Twesudde. Ibanda's enclosure appears to have been of considerable importance, for it lay just across a valley from the outposts of Bugabula
expansion from the southwest. In later decades, Ibanda achieved a few
victories over the people of Bugabula and established control of the lands
located just to the west of the northwest arm of the Nabisira.

the hand of Mukama Womunafu's "house" in the area. At the same time, the granting of estates to several of his sons endowed them with wealth and prestige and thereby permitted them to attract their own followers. In the long run, the growth of the community centering on Womunafu would be enhanced. The grant to Ibanda in the southwest would to a very great extent close off that area to intrusion from Bugabula, ultimately defusing a threat on the open frontier to the west.

The posting of these sons at various points in the neighborhood of Bukanga was in no way a spectacular innovation, though it did make possible a move to the new enclosure. These distributions to his sons followed the normative procedures of the princely families in the region: princes were to be settled among their mother's people. This had been the practice with Inhensiko's many sons, with Wambuzi's, and now with Womunafu's own young men. What the maintenance of this procedure does suggest is that despite existing outside the formal domain of Luuka, despite growing up in an enclosed world so very different from the playgrounds of his brothers, despite having around him a community composed of people from exceptionally diverse backgrounds who together attributed to him supernatural qualities, and despite having to respond to several new challenges on the northern margins of the Luuka state, the values upon which Mukama Womunafu based such dispositions were those of the conventional world.

The maintenance of values and norms intrinsic to the conventional world outside the enclosure suggests that the transformation of the focal personality within the enclosure was, in important ways, incomplete. The child Mukama was, indeed, vulnerable to the influence of ideas quite distinct from those that would affect his brothers who did not have the status of Mukama. By the 1850s, however, Mukama was no longer a child. While certain ideas could very

well be sustained in the enclosure, Mukama was now a
father. He had bound himself in a concrete way through
marriage ties with a number of families. He had a number of
children by various women who were wives as well as servants. The ideas that structured the Mukama persona fell
short of governing all these relationships. Mukama, his
wives, his children, his *bako*, could, in living these relationships, draw only or predominantly upon norms outside
the ideas and ideals of the enclosure—upon norms of the
conventional world at large. As his children matured, one
can suppose that these norms played ever increasing roles in
the daily life of the enclosure—governing the day-to-day relationships, the interactions of most of the people within.
To a very great extent these norms were in conflict with the
old ideas that sustained the heroic Mukama, which were
transmitted from one "Mukama node" to another: the
model of possessed leader; the "man on the move," "the
man whose figure joined this world and the other world,"
the "man who attracted numbers of followers" within a
climate of expectation.

Increasingly at Bukanga, one suspects, Mukama was
caught within a network of largely conventional relationships. In this, his capacity to act, to manipulate the Mukama
formula, to draw new people in, to challenge the power of
Nafa, was progressively impeded. The period of upheaval
that began about 1855, which brought a new wave of refugees within his grasp, provided Mukama with a magnifi-
cent opportunity to renew his stature, to retest his capacities
to attract new people into his service, to counteract the op-
pressive array of old relationships at Bukanga, to bring
closer the eclipse of Nafa. Twesudde was an opportunity
taken after a period of having been "held back."

VI

Womunafu and Nafa

THE struggle between Mukama Womunafu and Nafa extended over three decades. It was occasionally violent. Tradition records instances of people physically driven from the land, supporters of Nafa covered with ashes, pogroms against compounds in which Nafa's people were residing. These were the outer limits of the struggle. But at first the conflict appears to have been more effectively handled within the sphere of social relations. It has been noted how Mukama and his camp drew women away from Nafa's community and invested them in premier roles within the Bukanga enclosure.[1] It has been recorded that Mukama Womunafu gave his sister Napiri to a key elder living within Nafa's world and thereby structured a crucial relationship with an important family that was once within Nafa's grasp. Mukama Womunafu's later marriages at Bukanga to Kinaita, daughter of Butaho of the Mabandha clan, and to Nabirye, daughter of Wenswadhe of the Kabambwe clan, were symptomatic, if not causative, of a changing balance of power within the immediate area of Bunafu around mid-century. Butaho and Wenswadhe lived along the southwestern margins of Nafa's area, and these two marriages had the effect of strengthening Mukama Womunafu's own following while at the same time weakening the ties between Nafa and the families that had once acknowledged his power. This aggression in the field of *buko* alliances ultimately made possible the move from Bukanga to the new enclosure called Twesudde.

There is nothing extraordinary about such competition between leaders in this arena of marriage. The coalescence and maintenance of support from both inside and outside the community is fundamental to leadership. Communities in the region are in no way "natural growths" or extended patrilineages. They are social formations built up through marriage and clientship ties between and among core lineages (which may provide the leaders) and disparate individuals and groups (old settlers and new immigrants). Marriage, as has been noted, is significant because it is the one generator of social linkage over which man has entire control and which has a capacity to endure beyond the immediate moment, even beyond the generation of the spouses.[2] The competitive aspect is merely an extension and intensification of the application of interest, knowledge, and tactic to the *buko* network.

Because this was a world in which marriages were the key institutions of social linkage, historical data on marriage hold the potential for unveiling the larger and sometimes less visible dimensions of social groups and social networks in the past and, moreover, of the course of formation of these groups and networks. The marriage data survive time and change because the relationships have a tendency to persist (in the requirements of descendants to know their forbears). Other institutions of social linkage such as clientship and friendship—unless cemented in *buko* linkages and land and office allocations—have less capacity to generate data that may survive. The superior capacity of marriage data to be maintained over time gives a certain penumbra of bias to the body of evidence on the nature of the precolonial community. The reconstructed community is perceived as a composite of networks of marriage, and not as a field encompassing transitory as well as enduring relationships, which in reality it was.

The historical rendering of community is, therefore, imperfect, yet it does provide a glimpse of the "outer dimensions" of social networks and communities. The data on

124

marriage available from Bunafu indicate that the networks of social relationships centering on Nafa and Womunafu began to alter around the middle of the nineteenth century and that a deep and important cleavage opened up between the two networks. Before 1855, it has already been noted, lineages established within the domain of Nafa appear to have been encouraged to create *buko* ties with Mukama Womunafu at Bukanga. After 1855 and right through to the eclipse of Nafa around 1870, this was not true. There were no further *buko* ties between the old supporters of Nafa and the lineage of Womunafu. It was only a decade *after the collapse* of Nafa's authority that a member of Nafa's lineage renewed through marriage an old *buko* tie with one of the groups that had become affiliated with Mukama Womunafu. At no time was anyone from Mukama Womunafu's lineage ever joined in marriage to anyone from Nafa's lineage. The evidence suggests the emergence of a decisive social boundary in this period, a boundary between the two increasingly exclusive *buko* networks. In turn, the cleavage in networks suggests the existence in this period of a potent social barrier between the communities of Nafa and Womunafu. (See figure 5.)

While marriage was used effectively in the quiet struggle between Womunafu's and Nafa's spheres, it was not the only significant instrument used in the conflict. The evidence indicates that when Mukama evacuated Bukanga between 1855 and 1860, he and his new supporters attempted to use physical position to further the isolation of Nafa's lineage, to sterilize thereby Nafa's prominence. Mukama Womunafu and his new people could have selected any of a number of sites in the Bunafu area for a new enclosure. The fact that the one selected required quite extensive clearance of woodland—a task not necessary at Bukanga—suggests that the site was chosen neither by whim nor by accident but rather by design. Its location just above the lands of Nafa's

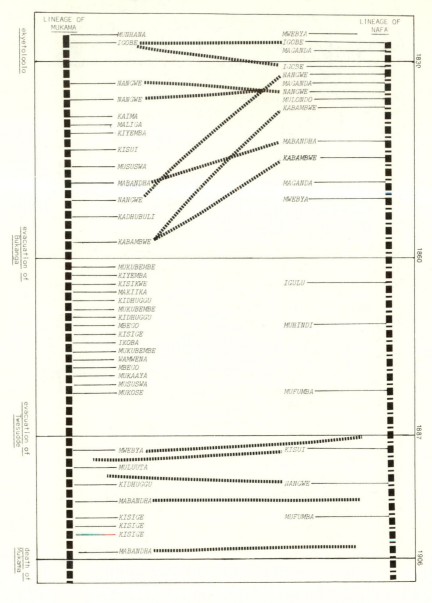

LINEAGE OF MUKAMA

LINEAGE OF NAFA

ekyetololo

MUNHANA
IGOBE
MWEBYA
IGOBE
MAGANDA

1830

IGOBE
NANGWE
MAGANDA
NANGWE
NANGWE
MILONDO
KABAMBWE

KAIMA
MALIGA
KIYEMBA

KISUI
MABANDHA

MUSUSWA
KABAMBWE

MABANDHA
MAGANDA

NANGWE
MWEBYA

KADHUBULI

evacuation of Bukanga

KABAMBWE

1860

MUKUBEMBE
KIYEMBA
KISIKWE
MAKIIKA
KIDHUGGU
MUKUBEMBE
KIDHUGGU
MBEGO
KISIGE
IKOBA
MUKUBEMBE
WAMWENA
MBEGO
MUKAAYA
MUSUSWA
MUKOSE
IGULU

MUHINDI

MUFUMBA

evacuation of Twesudde

1887

MWEBYA
KISUI

MULUUTA

KIDHUGGU
NANGWE

MABANDHA

KISIGE
KISIGE
MUFUMBA
KISIGE

death of Mukama

MABANDHA

1906

—— buko linkages ▮▮▮▮▮▮▮▮▮ linkages between buko networks

126

FIGURE 5 ● The Buko Networks of the Lineages of Mukama and Nafa. The figure presents a simplified model of the marriage linkages between members of the lineages of Mukama and Nafa and members of other lineages, noted here by name of clan. Marriages of people residing in the immediate neighborhood are noted while those of people who drifted away are omitted. For the lineage of Mukama, only marriages of Mukama and of his sons (but not of his grandsons) are noted, while for the lineage of Nafa the marriages of both sons and grandsons are included. Marriages organized after the death of Mukama in 1906 are omitted. The periodization and the sequences are approximate. What is revealed is a very distinctive cleavage between the *buko* networks of Nafa and Mukama emerging in the time of the occupation of the Twesudde enclosure between ca. 1855-60 and 1887.

own lineage suggests that the objective was to intensify the pressure on Nafa's lineage. (See map 16, chapter V.)

Twesudde may represent, for the distant observer, the shift of competition and conflict from the social field to that of physical position and survival. Twesudde was located almost immediately adjacent to the old compound of Womunafu's own mother's people: the Igobe. The Igobe groups at Bunafu had been securely a part of the small realm of Nafa, but from the early days at Twesudde, certainly, they were physically closer to the enclosure of Mukama. Twesudde was also sited on the sloping land between Nafa's own gardens and the compound of Kudhaiga's Nangwe people, effecting physically the separation of Nangwe groups from Nafa's community that had begun through *buko*. If the *kyonzira* had ever been cast so as to create a strong boundary between the worlds of Nafa and Mukama Womunafu, certainly by the time of Twesudde Mukama had overcome any constraints on his movements.

The move to Twesudde was to lead directly to the eclipse of Nafa. The enclosure cut off once and for all the lands to the north of Nafa's compound, the control of which had been firmly Nafa's at one time. Twesudde narrowed Nafa's leverage in respect to the distribution of land. Nafa's own lands on the lower hillslopes were isolated. Mukama's posi-

127

tion precluded the expansion of Nafa's extended family anywhere in the Bunafu area.

As a consequence of the disadvantageous position of Nafa after the erection of Twesudde, Nafa's capacity to maintain the support of his old followers' sons was in peril. Significantly, tradition provides no record of any refugees joining Nafa in the period of Luuka turbulence that began about 1855. Moreover, the 1860s were the period in which people of the Muganza clan, Nafa's very own lineage, began arriving in Bugabula from the Bunafu area. These were the children of Nafa Kidolo, who had witnessed the appearance of Mukama some quarter of a century earlier. These were the children of Nafa Kitubi, who had seen his support slip away to Bukanga. These men of the Muganza clan were either being forced from their lands or else were finding it impossible to get land given the constriction of opportunities within Nafa's shrinking world.[3]

If members of Nafa's own lineage were seeking out opportunities far away in Bugabula, the situation was most likely far worse for the remnants of Nafa's community. As noted, there were no further marriages between the remnants and the enclosure. What then were their choices— isolation, restriction, departure? People like Wagubona, the Mulondo man, and his wife Lubagu, daughter of Nafa, fled with their children to Bugabula where a huge expanse of country was open to settlement and where commoners were welcomed into high and low administrative offices throughout the country.[4]

In the second half of the nineteenth century, Bugabula maintained a strong and relatively stable political system. There was a very low incidence of princely conflict and, until the 1890s, there were no violent succession struggles. The key to this stability and to the capacity of the state to maintain the unity of the country was the short shrift given princes of the Bugabula royal family. Those princes were given few offices, and then minor ones, and allowed limited prerogative. Commoner men were invested in high offices and in most middle and lower offices in the administrative hierarchy. Commoners had license to summon, to arrest, and to discipline princes. Consequently, commoner groups found Bugabula a land of many political opportunities, and Bugabula became in the period from about 1840 to 1895, at least, a magnet for migrants and refugees from all over Busoga.[5]

If Bugabula then offered a pull, Luuka, at least between 1855 and 1870, provided the push. Luuka was at this time experiencing an "era of princes." During these years of turbulence, men of the ruling house of Luuka expressed claims of status and privilege apparently far broader than any expressed before. The elevation of princely prerogative in Luuka at a time when princes were being held in check in Bugabula created a significant distinction in commoner status between Bugabula and Luuka. This differential generated a considerable flow of commoners from all over Luuka toward Bugabula. This migrational trend did not make Luuka a kind of quiet backwater. In fact, as has been noted, Luuka was in this period an attractive place for refugees and adventurers who had lost their land, office, or patron in the states to the east. Many moved to Luuka seeking to take advantage of the civil disturbances there, hoping to join a successful prince or campaign. There were also many migrations within Luuka, which had the effect of relieving commoner groups of the distress felt in one place, at least in the short term. The point here is that between about 1855 and 1870 there was a decided trend toward Bugabula.[6] Luuka may not have lost much of its total population in the balance, but it lost much of its seasoned base. The newcomers, coming from areas in which princely prerogative was unchecked and seeking to advance the position of one or another prince in Luuka, tended to exacerbate the tensions

within Luuka. These commoner men and women from the
east, over just a few years, may very well have effected a
change in the nature of princely rights in Luuka, allowing
princes to operate in their own spheres without significant
challenge.

Retrospectively, it appears that even before the beginnings of turbulence in Luuka politics in the 1850s, Mukama
was able to overwhelm Nafa. Yet, perhaps significantly, the
final phase of attack on Nafa came at a time when princes of
the Luuka royal house were exercising their privileges right
across the land. In important aspects Mukama Womunafu
was different from all the other contemporaneous princes of
Luuka, but in this period Mukama was operating as one
among many. That Nafa's eclipse coincided with the increasing deployment of princely prerogative across the
whole of Luuka is one of a bundle of indications that
Mukama Womunafu was becoming a part of the wider
Luuka world, responsive to its styles, interests, and
changes.

By 1870, Nafa was no longer a challenge to Womunafu.
What remained of Nafa's world were his own children and
the few occupants of the lower hillslopes who were living
on land apparently still unattractive to Womunafu and his
following. Nafa Kyotaite moved to a small fenced enclosure
on the margins of the Nakaibaale swamp.[7] In 1971, several
informants remarked that the name "Nafa" meant, simply,
"and there it ended,"[8] appropriate, if somewhat anachronis-
tic. To illuminate the proffered etymology further, one can
note that there were in 1971 some 445 living descendants of
Mukama Womunafu of his patrilineage living in Bunafu.
There were but six descendants of the patrilineage of Nafa
living in Bunafu, and but two were adults.[9]

VII

Reflections of a Wider World

BY the early 1870s, Mukama Womunafu was entirely
secure on the *mutala*. The story of the eclipse of Nafa
was complete. The traditions suggest, however, that Mukama's community was no longer an enclosed domain, a
world separate and different from the larger world around it.
The Twesudde enclosure imitated in style not the Bukanga
enclosure but rather the single-gated enclosure of its day.
(See figure 6.) The presence of but one gate is unexplained
in tradition, though what is known of the period provides
one line of explanation. This was a period in which there

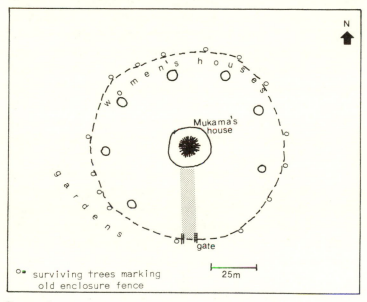

FIGURE 6 • Approximate Plan of Twesudde Enclosure

131

was a scourge of kidnapping across much of Busoga. Kidnappers sought victims to carry to Buganda to serve the big men of that kingdom or to send along the routes of the long-distance slave trade which funneled human traffic to the East African coast. Baganda and Basoga alike participated in the kidnapping and transport of slaves. No place in Busoga was hallowed sanctuary after about 1850.[1]

In particular there was a great demand in Buganda for women from east of the Nile. Ganda men relished the supposed attributes of women from Busoga, finding their elegantly cicatriced bodies beautiful and their separation from the tense, competitive arenas of Ganda politics a great virtue. There were like demands for women at the courts of Busoga. Rulers across much of northern Busoga sought beautiful women from outside their domains, and they awarded generously the parties of kidnappers who brought back attractive women to their courts. Even today many people in Busoga recall their adventurous antecedents who romped over Busoga in pursuit of women for their chiefs. This new "sport" generated enormous fear in the compounds of people all across Busoga. The fear of losing wives and daughters may not have been the only reason for closing up or eliminating the wives' gate from the enclosure during this era, but no other explanation for this architectural change emerges from what is known of the region in this period.

The one gate of Twesudde aligned directly south toward the capital of Luuka, suggesting that by 1855 or so the relations of Mukama's community to the rulers of Luuka had become deferential. If the new enclosure was in fact a symbol of the regeneration of the community, the old ideal of isolation from the political world had disappeared. There was by this time little possibility that an important person, particularly a prince, could opt out of the larger world. There are several reasons for this. The years from 1855 to

1870 were clearly turbulent. When the central administration was under control, it was only through the mastery of office by one or another of the sons of Wambuzi, principally Kalogo and Kibalya. They successively seized the throne and preempted the succession of Kakuku's eldest son Mudhungu and thereby threw into disarray the old ideal of paternal succession.[2] Once that ideal was thrown into question, the potential claimants to the throne grew enormously. This was the era of princes, and competing brothers of Kakuku sought help from near and far to strengthen their positions within the state, to extend their influence beyond the local communities in which they resided. Kalogo and Kibalya sought Ganda help to sort out their opponents, to deal out reprisals against those people in Luuka who they thought were in opposition to the throne.[3]

This was a period in which support was won community by community through force of arms or threat of violence. Luuka was not created by conquest, but between 1855 and 1870 it was increasingly maintained by force. Because of this, it was a period in which deferential behavior constituted the strongest protection against attack and reprisal. This would have been particularly so for those communities controlled by the brothers of Kalogo and Kibalya, for the siblings of these rulers stood in the front line of suspects. Mukama Womunafu was, of course, a younger brother of Kalogo and Kibalya, and the deference expressed toward these two princes in the form of the alignment of the Twesudde gate may have been one of the ways in which Mukama's people short-circuited suspicions about his activities north of the Nabisira, about his independence, about his particular capacities to attract support.

But if outward deference was displayed toward the Luuka courts, there is evidence of at least one other focus of interest. The 1860s and 1870s were a period in which the Bulamogi kingdom to the north took increasing interest in the lands north of the Nabisira. Settlers loyal to the Bulamogi throne moved steadily across the weakly marked frontiers between the heartland of Bulamogi and this northern tier above the Nabisira which was not yet fully integrated by Luuka.[4] This tier constituted one segment of a wider band of territory of great attractiveness stretching from west of the Nile River to the foothills of Mount Elgon in the east. The Buganda kingdom was encouraging settlement in what is now called Bugerere during this period. A large number of *kitongole* grants were made there by the Kabaka and by other officials of the Ganda state.[5] Across the Nile to the east, the capitals of Bugabula were shifting north toward the more open lands of north-central Busoga. Still farther east, the Luuka capitals were shifting northward toward the Nabisira. Throughout the nineteenth century, the Bulamogi capitals were shifting steadily south and west from their earlier locations close to the Mpologoma River, and the region of what is today northern Luuka was brought into a far more attractive proximity to the Bulamogi state. The capitals of Busiki in the northeast too were shifting southwestward toward this band of attractive land. The Buzimba core of the Kigulu state system was also apparently interested, for its headquarters moved northward toward an enhanced accessibility to this zone. (See map 17.)

This noteworthy shift of attention toward this open land in the nineteenth century appears to be more than just the result of developments long underway, more than a consequence of a search for better land for cultivation, more than an escape hatch for groups worn down by the play of Ganda hegemony in the south-central areas. This new region—if a band of territory some twelve kilometers across and twenty kilometers long can be called such—linked up directly with what is today called "the Nyoro trade." This trade in salt, iron, cattle, and slaves connected centers of production and markets around the Lake Kyoga basin to markets more directly under the control of the Bunyoro kingdom. The trade entered the Busoga region from Lake Kyoga or across the Nile and then worked south and east to several points of collection and distribution located along this belt. Markets in Busoga linked up with centers of demand and with hunting groups east of Busoga. (See map 17.)

This northern or Nyoro trade had not always been important, but in the second half of the nineteenth century it was becoming more vital to the Busoga region as a whole. The old and important production areas, markets, and trade ties close by the Lake Victoria littoral of southern Busoga were coming under terrible pressure as a consequence of Ganda attempts to monopolize the Lake trade.[6] The northern market network gradually supplanted the southern network in the second half of the nineteenth century. This shift is particularly noteworthy in the iron trade. Where iron in the form of hoe blades had previously been brought into central Busoga from the Samia region southeast of Busoga and by way of the Lake Victoria coastlands of southern Busoga, by the 1850s the Nyoro hoe had almost completely replaced the Samia hoe in the markets of central Busoga.

The most important Soga markets for the Nyoro trade were located within this relatively narrow band of land. Kagulu was the key entrepôt south of Lake Kyoga and became the focus for economic activity in Bugabula through the latter part of the nineteenth century. To the southeast lay Nawaka, another important market site. Nawaka was located in an area not under the control of Luuka and not within the formal control of Bulamogi. But the Nyoro trade and the Nawaka market in particular were good reasons for the simultaneous expansion of Bulamogi and Luuka influence in this region north of the Nabisira between 1860 and 1877.

It was not only along a frontier of competitive expansion that Luuka and Bulamogi interests touched. Mudhungu,

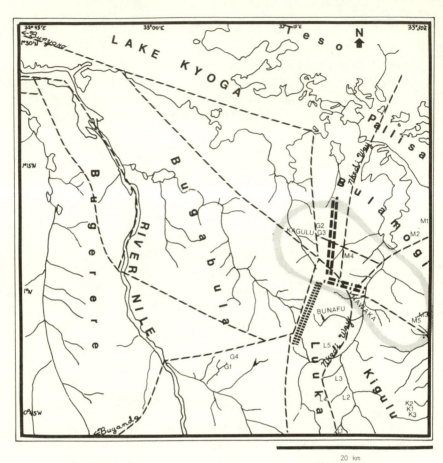

20 km

MAP 17 ● A New Region of Interest. There are various indications that in the second half of the nineteenth century the rulers of Bugabula, Luuka, and Bulamogi began to shift their attention from the environs of their old capitals to a region lying just north of the Nabisira. It was within, or adjacent to, this region that some of the great battles of the last decades of the precolonial era were fought. It was within this area that the market centers of Kagulu and Nawaka were located. The important pathways of trade, migration, and communication went through this zone. Along such routes as the "Nkedi Way" passed ideas of northern cast to the south. In the latter part of the nineteenth century, this region (roughly denoted on the map but certainly not confined by any boundary) became a magnet for settlers coming from several directions. One explanation is that this area became attractive for settlement and trade as the Lake Victoria trade (particularly in iron goods) in southern Busoga collapsed and the Nyoro trade in iron goods from the north and west came increasingly to substitute for it. As Kagulu and Nawaka lay along the principal paths, they benefited from this wholesale shift of trade northward in this period.

▊▊▊▊▊▊▊▊▊ ▊▊▊▊▊▊▊▊▊	the fronts of Bugabula-Luuka warfare in the late nineteenth century
▪▬▪▬▪▬	the fronts of Luuka-Bulamogi warfare in the late nineteenth century
▬▬▬▬▬▪ ▪▬▬▬▬	the fronts of Bugabula-Bulamogi warfare in the late nineteenth century
▬ ▬ ▬ ▬	approximate locations of principal pathways in late nineteenth century northern Busoga
	the general location of this "new region of interest"

Principal Capitals in northern Busoga
(in sequence)

Bugabula

G1 Kagoda at Naminage
G2 Kitamirike I at Kagulu
G3 Kadhumbula I at Kagulu
G4 Mutiibwa at Naminage

Luuka

L1 Kakuku at Kiroba
L2 Kalogo at Nabitama
L3 Kibalya at Naigobya
L4 Mudhungu at Kiyunga
L5 Inhensiko II at Bulalu

Bulamogi

M1 Wako at Mpambwa
M2 Wako at Gadumire
M3 Kisira at Kaliro
M4 Kisira at Nawaikoke
M5 Wambuzi at Natwana

Kigulu/Buzimba

K1 Walusansa at Nasuuti
K2 Gologolo at Nasuuti
K3 Miro at Nasuuti

who succeeded Kibalya as the ruler of Luuka in 1870, had sent his young son Nabwana to the Bulamogi court for safekeeping and instruction in the ways of government, much as his father had sent him to be raised in the Bugabula court. Even before Mudhungu's accession to the throne, his supporters in Luuka commonly communicated with the Bulamogi court on the matter of Nabwana's upbringing and on the question of Mudhungu's claim to the Luuka throne. The attentions of important commoners in Luuka and of Mukama Womunafu toward the Bulamogi capital were facilitated by the development of a "safe" road from the northern bank of the Nabisira up through Nawaka and then

137

northeastward to the Bulamogi capital. This road was, not
surprisingly, called *Nkedi*—the route of the Bakedi, the
route of the "northern people," the "Bulamogi way." Directed up this road were the attentions of dissident groups in
Luuka. Down this road filtered ideas and styles from the
north. (See map 17.) It was during the 1870s that Mukama
Womunafu, for example, began to emulate the important
men of Bulamogi by wearing *nfuluutu* on his wrists and
ankles. These were heavy iron rings, the wearing of which
was a fashion spreading south from well north of the Mpologoma River. Nabwana, Mudhungu's son, would later
wear them in the capital of Luuka—when he was brought
from Bulamogi in 1877 or 1878 to succeed his father as
ruler of Luuka.[7]

The horizons of Bunafu, of Womunafu's small community, had then widened dramatically since the last days at
Bukanga. If in the earlier period the role of father had ir-
resistibly impinged on the ideals of the enclosed life of a
Mukama figure, now it was the world at large that began to
make it increasingly more difficult for Mukama and his
close men and women to sustain the original ideals of the
isolated, enclosed, heroic Mukama. Long-distance political
and economic contacts were becoming more decisive in the
lives of the peoples right across the lands north of the Nabisira. The home of Kabalu's kin just meters to the east of
Twesudde was the meeting place for commoner leaders who
sought to rid the country of King Kibalya and to install
Mudhungu on the throne. Kabalu's compound, and the region north of the Nabisira generally, was in closer contact
with the great cosmopolitan court of Buganda as the 1860s
wore on. Just several kilometers to the east of Bunafu lived
the Muluuta men who had served as chiefly representatives
of the Luuka state north of the Nabisira. For the most part,
the Muluuta leaders supported Mudhungu and thus made
more difficult the integration of the region north of the

Nabisira into the Luuka state during the era of Kalogo and Kibalya. But what is significant here about these Muluuta folk is that Muluuta men and their aides and servants from the area of Budhuuba on the Nabisira visited Buganda many times (See map 4, chapter I). Through the middle third of the nineteenth century they rubbed shoulders with other travelers at the Buganda court: representatives from African courts to the west and south, Arab and Swahili traders from the East African coast, and European explorers. Before the close of the Twesudde period, one Muluuta man would travel as far as Buddu, a western region of Buganda some 250 kilometers from the banks of the Nabisira, and return to Budhuuba.[8]

King Kibalya was removed in 1870, and Mudhungu was brought from Bugabula and seated on the throne of Luuka. The long cabal of the commoners had achieved its objective. Mudhungu's reign, which lasted until 1877, would be a brief era in which commoners held tremendous power within the state. They set Mudhungu on the throne, and they did not release their grip on the affairs of state for something like a decade. They disciplined the unruly and rebellious princes across the countryside and invigorated the offices of territorial chiefs in the administration of the domain. These commoner offices had been created by Inhensiko I and had been maintained by Wambuzi. They had come under attack during the era of the princes—that is, during the reigns of Kalogo and Kibalya. In fact, virtually all the holders of the highest commoner offices in the Luuka state were executed in Buganda in the "feces affair." During the era of princes, their sons and successors would have been extremely cautious in the exercise of territorial authority and restrained in adventure in the affairs of the Luuka state. The high incidence of civil war made their relations with rulers potentially deadly, certainly tentative and unstable. Mudhungu was the only prince on the horizon who could be advanced

toward the throne without necessarily extending and intensifying the era of princes. Mudhungu's accession would
mean a restoration of a narrow succession pattern. It was
perhaps because of this that so many of those who had been
suddenly and tragically invested in their fathers' offices after
the feces affair followed a path toward the compound of the
late Kabalu. Kabalu's kin remained the stable pinion within
the Luuka state and the foremost supporters of Mudhungu's
claims to the throne.

So, with Mudhungu's accession, the era of princes suddenly ended. During the 1870s Mudhungu and his commoner chiefs erected a system in which commoners were
given extensive responsibility and princes close scrutiny. It
was during this period in Bunafu that Mukama Womunafu
himself appointed a commoner, Bawalamayi, as a *katikkiro*
or *kitwikiro*.[9] Bawalamayi was a man of the Mwebya clan
and, although from outside Bunafu, was a member of the
Mwebya lineage that once had supported Nafa but had eventually come within the circle of Mukama. Significantly,
Bawalamayi came from one of the lineages of the great
commoner chiefs of Luuka of the day: that of Nagaya of
Nawansega.[10]

Bawalamayi was entrusted with the management of the
day-to-day affairs of the enclosure and the supervision of
the activities of the princely children and grandchildren of
Womunafu. The traditions from Bunafu suggest that previously Mukama Womunafu had, to the extent he desired it,
been served in these capacities by religious specialists, the
skilled practitioners of spirit possession, divination, and
healing who had surrounded the Mukama from his birth.
Now, with the appointment of Bawalamayi, Mukama Womunafu appears to have shifted course dramatically. Here
was an outsider, someone from beyond the world of the enclosure, someone closely attached to the political world of
Luuka. Here was this Mwebya man, an "administrative

specialist," brought in to supervise the insiders, the princes, the old followers, the earnest religious enthusiasts.

Mukama Womunafu's appointment of Bawalamayi in the 1870s reflects his readiness to reach beyond the small Bunafu community and touch the ideas and institutions of the larger Luuka state. Within Bunafu he was introducing an institution—the great commoner chief—found in the 1870s to be of importance in the maintenance of the upper levels of administration of the kingdom. Beyond suggesting that Mukama may have become more open to ideas appearing within the Luuka kingdom in the era of Mudhungu, the appointment of the commoner to this position of authority suggests that Mukama Womunafu was shifting his role from that of the heroic pastoralist figure in an isolated and enclosed world toward that of an active participant in the affairs of the broader society. Mukama Womunafu not only established this commoner as his chief aide but also in these years gave daughters to two divisional chiefs of Luuka: Waiduuba Pokino of Budhuuba, chief of the northern area, and Nagaya of Nawansega, chief of the central.[11]

The relationship between Mukama and the Mwebya lineage was reinforced about 1887 when Mukama left Twesudde and built a new enclosure some thousand meters southeast of the Twesudde site. The new enclosure was called *Bwebya* because it was snuggled among old settlements of the Mwebya lineage on the hillslopes. In moving to Bwebya, Mukama abandoned not only the areas of Bunafu thickly settled by princes and by his early supporters, he also abandoned the ridge environment for the lusher and better-drained slopes that had once been the niche of Nafa's people. (See map 18.)

Bwebya was a commoner world and remains so today as one of the subvillages (*bisoko*) in Bunafu with the highest concentration of commoner residents. At the time of the erection of the enclosure these lands were occupied by the

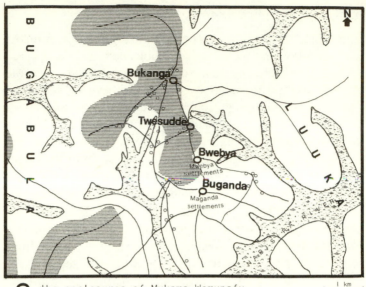

○   the enclosures of Mukama Womunafu

━━ the approximate locations of important paths
in late nineteenth-century Bunafu

○ the approximate locations of households of
Mukama Womunafu's patrilineage around the time
of Mukama's death in 1906

     ridge, at least 1,100
     meters above sea level

     river and stream valleys
     below 1,070 meters above
     sea level

MAP 18 ● To Bwebya and Then to Buganda. About 1887, Mukama
Womunafu ended his long residence at Twesudde and moved into his
new enclosure at Bwebya. Bwebya was located to the south, on lower
ground, and among the compounds of the Mwebya groups who were related to Bawalamayi, Mukama's *kitwikiro*. But the occupation of
Bwebya was brief, and by 1892 Mukama had evacuated Bwebya for a
new enclosure farther south near the Maganda households on the lower
slopes of the *mutala*. The enclosure was called Buganda and brought
Mukama Womunafu still closer to the palace of Nabwana Inhensiko II of
Luuka at Bulalu, a few kilometers to the south. Buganda was Mukama's
last enclosure, and it was there that his funeral was celebrated in 1906,
and it is there that he is buried.

142

Mwebya people and by several groups that traced their origins back to the coastlands of Lake Victoria. When Mukama moved from Bukanga to Twesudde, he sought to complement the old support from his family of princes and early supporters. In moving from Twesudde to Bwebya, Mukama appears to have rejected entirely his own lineage.

Such a postulated tension between Mukama Womunafu and his own growing lineage would not be at variance with what has been observed of mid-twentieth-century Busoga. Lloyd Fallers, who studied the political institutions of late colonial Busoga, saw the conflict between chief and his own family as a key element within political life. Fallers attempted to unveil and to understand the tension existing between the ruler (or headman or chief) and the members of his own lineage living within his domain, kin who shared the ruler's status but whose ambitions had to be limited and could be limited through the sharing of authority between ruler and commoner. Fallers wrote:

> The ruler himself was both the head of the state hierarchy and a member of the royal clan and lineage. His unique position at the head of the state was, however, in conflict with his membership in the royal company of equals. If he emphasised his link with his commoner clients, he violated lineage values. If he did not, he stood in danger of losing his paramount authority to his lineage-mates. Similar conflicts today, and presumably also in the past, afflict the hereditary village headman. He also had to balance territorial headship against lineage membership and thus might become involved in conflict with his lineage-mates.[12]

This view of conflict in role and status also makes sense in terms of what is known of the history of the royal family in the Luuka area in the 1870s and 1880s. The Luuka state was in the 1870s attempting to cope with the problem of princely prerogatives, which had been extensively invoked during the previous decade or two. The 1870s constituted a period of reaction against the princes who were seen to be de-

stabilizing influences in the country after the execution of
Kakuku. The ruler, Mudhungu, attempted to use his big
commoner chiefs—the *bakungu*—to discipline and control
princes who invoked excessive prerogative. Mudhungu
gave out little largesse to the princes. Instead, he used the
offices, titles, and gifts that he had the power to dispense to
draw more commoners into Luuka and to strengthen the positions of the commoner chiefs.

Such a tension within the royal family (between ruler and
his kin, for example) is further suggested by the rates of
growth of the Luuka royal family in this period. The era of
Mudhungu was the third generation after Inhensiko I's. The
princely lineages of Inhensiko's many sons as well as those
of Wambuzi's children were seeking more and more land on
which to settle.[13] Various students of royal families in Africa have noted that royalty reproduce themselves at a considerably more rapid rate than the nonroyal people around
them because of differing rates of polygyny.[14] In turn, this
imbalance in the rates of growth of royal and nonroyal
groups, while enhancing the capacity of the royal group to
dominate, places constraints upon the holder of central authority. Sons wish to bear the prestige and titles of, or similar to, their fathers. Their demands for grants of land, titles,
and offices may place intolerable pressure on the state's resources. What is significant about the reign of Mudhungu is
that in spite of (indeed, in reaction to) these pressures, the
balance of influence tilted away from princes and toward the
commoners.

A similar situation appears to have developed in Bunafu.
There, over some forty years, the lineage of princes in Bunafu was experiencing extremely rapid growth. Womunafu
had twenty-six sons who survived to maturity. All of these
sons were born before 1893, and all but three of them had
children. The thirteen sons who were born in the first enclosure at Bukanga and survived to maturity alone had some
forty-one sons who survived to maturity. By the 1870s and

1880s, then, the royal lineage in Bunafu—the lineage of Mukama Womunafu—was undergoing an astonishing rate of population growth, one unequaled among the lineages in the northern part of Luuka.[15] Such a rate of growth transformed the nature of Bunafu. The children and grandchildren of Mukama Womunafu placed fantastic demands upon the head of the community. These demands stimulated conflicts with firmly settled commoners whose only defense against the land hunger of the princes was the intervention of Mukama Womunafu himself. One may postulate that Mukama Womunafu, in attempting to deal with these situations, found himself torn between a group or groups of commoners who were earnest in their support of Mukama and perceived him as a leader of great prestige and a growing group of kinsmen who perceived Mukama more as a member of their family, a father or grandfather, less an exceptional leader of great and unusual elevation, one prince among many.

Mukama Womunafu had no infinite base of resources. Much of what he did have had been passed to his sons Ibanda, Nhiro, Galya, and Lwaidho, who themselves were using these grants to create their own circles of prestige and power on the northern, southern, and western areas of the *mutala*.[16] Mukama's role as prestigious intermediary between this world and another and as grantor of refuge had wilted with the inexorable loss of isolation, the breakup of the enclosed world. Moreover, Mukama's role as convener of a family of princely elevation was shaken by growing tensions between his role as leader of a lineage group and as leader of a community that extended beyond the boundaries of that lineage. Not surprisingly, about 1887 Mukama chose a solution most commonly adopted by leaders right across the Lake Victoria region: he walked away from the conflict at Twesudde. Moving away with Bawalamayi he built the new enclosure at Bwebya and settled among a new group of supporters—virtually all commoners.

145

VIII

The Bwebya Illness

As briefly noted, the heyday of commoner influence in Bunafu began in the 1870s with the appointment of Bawalamayi and was significantly reinforced with the movement of Mukama Womunafu and Bawalamayi to the new Bwebya enclosure about 1887. For the wider Luuka society, the era of the commoner began some years earlier with the installation of Mudhungu on the throne about 1870 and also closed earlier.

In the 1870s, as we have seen, Mudhungu and his commoner chiefs disciplined the princes right across Luuka. Some were censured, some subinfeudated, and others pillaged. Mukama Womunafu was apparently not attacked. He had given daughters to two of the great commoner chiefs of the day, and he appears to have maintained his deferential posture toward the Luuka court.

But one prince who was pillaged was Wambuzi Kyobe of Naigobya. Kyobe fled to Buganda. There he assembled a small raiding party composed for the most part of Basoga serving around the Ganda courts.[1] This party attacked Mudhungu's palace at Kiyunga in 1877, and Mudhungu himself was seriously wounded. Fearing his early death and possibly the reeruption of fratricide in Luuka, Mudhungu asked for his son Nabwana to be brought from Bulamogi and to be given the throne. Mudhungu's commoner chiefs raced to Bulamogi and brought back the young man who had been living in Bulamogi from soon after his birth (1858 or 1859).[2] He was seated on the stool of Luuka as Nabwana Inhensiko II in 1877 while Mudhungu was still alive.

146

If the great commoner chiefs and councilors of Mudhungu thought that the maintenance of filial succession
meant a continuity in policy, they were greatly mistaken.
Nabwana Inhensiko II was a man very different from his
father Mudhungu. He had been brought up in the palaces of
Wako I and Kisira, the Bulamogi rulers during the second
half of the nineteenth century.Tradition records that he arrived from Bulamogi wearing the fashionable *nfuluutu* (iron
rings) on his wrists and on his ankles and had the manners
and bearing of a prince of Bulamogi.[3] While over the previous several decades Mudhungu and his councilors had been
much a part of the expansive cultural realm centering on the
courts and manners of Buganda and Bugabula, Nabwana
had been raised in a country that up to the 1880s had had
little contact with either Bugabula or Buganda. Rather,
Bulamogi had close ties to the lands to the north. These
were the lands of Pallisa and southern Teso across the
Mpologoma River. It was in this northern region that the
Bulamogi rulers sought settlers and soldiers to strengthen
their control at home and to counter the intervention of
Buganda to the south and west. A steady flow of travelers,
hunters, soldiers, and migrants crossing the Mpologoma
kept Pallisa and Bulamogi in close contact. Bulamogi, in
fact, made strong claims to control the Pallisa region. It was
from Pallisa and Teso that the fashion of the *nfuluutu* had
come.[4] Certainly, more fashions and manners than this
crossed the Mpologoma, though it is understandable today
that references in tradition to less tangible aspects of culture
than iron rings would be scant. Even after some eighty years
of close interaction with the other former states of modern
Busoga District, Bulamogi remains a country very much
apart: in its ways of seeing the external world, in its ways of
perceiving and using a record of the past, in dialect, in politics, and in manners.

In one very significant way Bulamogi was certainly different from the societies of Bugabula and Luuka to the southwest and south. In Bulamogi, in the period between approximately 1860 and 1890, commoners held very few offices of importance in the state. Princes had extensive prerogatives, and the statuses of prince and commoner appear to have been sharply demarcated at the time.

Within the region, the realm in which Nabwana was raised could not have been more different from that in which his father Mudhungu had been raised. Bulamogi gave little preference to commoners.[5] They were not trusted with power. Given this, it is not surprising that just a few years after Nabwana Inhensiko II's accession, the first signs of a wholesale change of policy in Luuka became evident. Between about 1885 and 1900, hundreds of commoner families fled Luuka, their property having been pillaged and their offices seized by princes of the expanding royal family. Only one commoner, Muziramulungi (Inhensiko II's *katikkiro*), was granted village office in this period. More than twenty commoner lineages were divested of village offices.[6] Inhensiko II's role in this growing attack against commoner power was not merely passive; he encouraged the process through the redistribution of land and the investiture of princes in many important offices in Luuka.

The effects of this change of policy are observable in the Bunafu of the 1890s. Bwebya, symbolizing the "marriage" between commoner and ruler in the affairs of Bunafu, was abandoned in 1892 after a brief five-year occupation. Bwebya had been the "moment" of the commoners in a society in which commoners were increasingly given short shrift. The Bwebya period is remembered today by the princes of Bunafu as a time of great unhappiness. Tradition records that there was much illness in the enclosure, that few children were born there, that even fewer survived. Tradition relates that Womunafu lost one daughter, Bwenene, to

148

some Baganda kidnappers who passed through in 1892. Tradition reports that Womunafu himself was very sick there. Bwebya was evacuated as an "unhealthy place," and a new enclosure was erected 900 meters to the south.[7] Bawalamayi and apparently the whole notion of an active commoner *katikkiro* were left behind at Bwebya. That aspect of the Bwebya illness was apparently cured.

The new enclosure was called Buganda and was the largest of the four enclosures built for Mukama on Bunafu *mutala*. It was called Buganda not because it was erected in a period in which Ganda influence in the affairs of Busoga was at its height but rather because it was located in the neighborhood of compounds of the Maganda lineages on the lower hillslopes not far from the Nabisira. (See map 14, chapter V.) Because of the presence of Maganda folk there, the neighborhood had come to be known as Buganda. And the name passed to the enclosure.

Buganda, in design, was a complete departure from Bwebya and Twesudde. It was ovoid in shape, imitative of the great palace of Nabwana Inhensiko II built at Bulalu some years earlier, that palace almost certainly an imitation of the great palaces of the day in Buganda. The houses inside Buganda enclosure were arranged rectilineally rather than in a circular style. Another change from Bwebya and Twesudde was that the enclosure had, like Bukanga, two gates. (See figure 7.) Mukama called his large beehive-shaped house in the enclosure *Isimba*, meaning "freedom."[8]

The ovoid design and rectilinear organization of Buganda enclosure suggests that by the 1890s Mukama Womunafu himself had been fully integrated into the life of the Luuka state. The enclosure was no longer a place that separated Mukama from the wider world nor did it enclose him in a life different from the lives of other princes. The enclosure had become merely the architectural garment of a princely

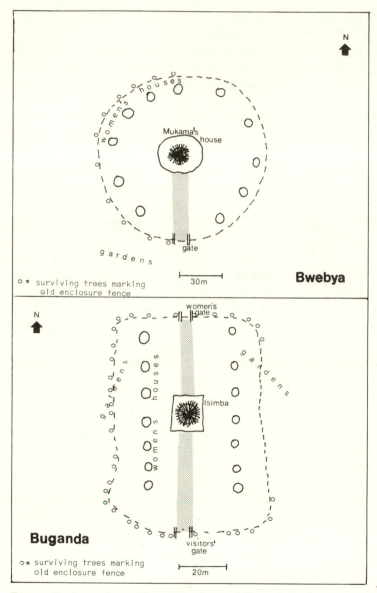

FIGURE 7 ● Approximate Plans of Bwebya and Buganda Enclosures

status. He was a prince not isolated from but rather joined to
the palace of a ruler who gave pronounced favor to princes,
a ruler who gave emphasis to the meaning of *mulangira* and
gave unity to the disparate collection of people called
balangira: the princes. Mukama had been singled out as exceptional at birth. By the 1890s he was one of many.

In his Isimba house, Mukama was no longer living on the
frontier of the Luuka kingdom. That frontier was by 1892
some twenty kilometers to the north. The capital of Luuka
had also shifted north. Inhensiko II had built a palace at
Bulalu north of the Kamirantumbu River. (See map 17,
chapter VII.) The *mbwa*-fly belt had by 1880 reached the
southern bank of the Kamirantumbu, and Inhensiko was determined to establish a headquarters comfortably beyond the
mbwa belt. Consequently, the Bulalu palace lay only about
ten kilometers south of Mukama Womunafu's Buganda enclosure. Mukama's children and grandchildren made frequent visits to Inhensiko's court, and many important
people visited the Buganda enclosure when traveling north
and south.

The move to Buganda, while it left behind the experience
of close alliance with commoner families, did not revitalize
the old man. Mukama had no children in Buganda who survived, though many women continued to serve him in the
palace, and children and grandchildren did stay with him
there. Tradition provides little data on this last residence
and last phase of Mukama's life.

In 1892, British agents established their first hold on what
was to become the District of Busoga, but which at the time
was just a collection of autonomous and semiautonomous
states, many subordinate to Buganda. Some men of Mukama's rank, though few of his age, were to gain immensely
from close participation in the early British activities in the
region, from the emerging "partnership" between the big
men of Busoga and the representatives of *Kwiini* Vic-

toria—but not Womunafu. The early impact of England on
Bunafu was seen in the baptism of Mukama's sixth son
Ibanda as Petero and in the introduction and rapid expansion
of cotton production in the Bunafu area.

Mukama Womunafu died in 1906, and his grave was
later cemented and inscribed in the modern style. The first
prince born in the village of Bunafu after Mukama
Womunafu's death was Petero's son. He was named
Mukama Womunafu. In 1971, there were some 445 descendants of Mukama Womunafu living in Bunafu. Few
members of Mukama's lineage had left Bunafu for other
areas or for the modernizing sectors of town and industry. It
was a royal *mutala*.

IX

Bunafu

GENERAL histories of nineteenth-century Africa are organized around the great courts of African monarchs, around the campsites of travelers from Europe, around the incidents of contact between an expansive Europe and a not uninterested Africa, around missions and ports, and around the great market places within which the presence of Europe was becoming increasingly commercial. Historians of Africa, like the explorers of a century ago, have been drawn from court to court, toward the headwaters of documentation, toward figures and places that project their own criteria of importance. This volume has followed a different path. It is a study of a small community in the Lake Victoria region of East Africa in the nineteenth century, a community called Bunafu, and it is a study of the career of Prince Womunafu, who came to dominate that community.

Bunafu was quite distant from the closest of the great courts of Africa, the court of Kabaka Mutesa I of Buganda, a court that attracted the emissaries of great nations, explorers, missionaries, and adventurers. Bunafu was remote from all this. Bunafu first felt the impact of missionaries some three decades after missionaries reached Mutesa's palace in 1877. Bunafu's soil was not touched by a European until the twentieth century. And it was a decade after Uganda was brought securely within the British colonial world as a protectorate that Bunafu first felt the impact of the world demand for cotton, a demand that would transform the local economy of Bunafu in the twentieth century, completing the "channeling" of the regional economy.

153

Even within its region—the modern District of Busoga —the personalities and events associated with Bunafu command little attention today. It is not only that local history is barely touched in the schools of the district, but also that Prince Womunafu's field of authority extended over no more than about twenty square kilometers, one neighborhood within a kingdom, one prince among many who held office as heads of village estates. Prince Womunafu was a Mukama—a possessed figure of heightened prestige—yet here again he was one among several princely figures accorded this distinctive status.

Given the nature of the evidence, even a reconstruction that brings this prince, Mukama Womunafu, to the center of the historian's field of vision generates only the simplest career profile. The profile could be recapitulated in a very few words.

Mukama Womunafu was a prince—thought to be possessed. He came from Makutu as a young child with a coterie of supporters, was settled into the first of four enclosures that he occupied in Bunafu, had many wives and children, achieved a position of dominance in the Bunafu area, and died in 1906.

This study is then clearly not concerned with the "importance of things," nor is it concerned with rehabilitating those anonymous and inarticulate folk who at best appear on occasion in very dim outline on the horizon of history. And while the simple reconstruction presented here tends to be oriented around what are taken to be four key developments—the formation and growth of a coterie, the expansion and performance of Mukama's lineage, the progress of Mukama through four enclosures, and the eclipse of an earlier headman—the study is not solely a reconstruction. More pointedly, it is very much an exploration—for it attempts to understand some aspects of another world from

154

the footing of a narrow path. It is an exploration of the nature and limits of the evidence of, and on, the past. It is an exploration of precolonial society. It is an exploration of the nature and significance of geographical mobility among a population in the past. It is an exploration of the nature of community in one setting. More particularly, it is an exploration of authority—of the modes and character of royal domination in the precolonial society and of the play of an authority formula, *Mukama*, in a specific and narrow context.

In some ways, such a community as Bunafu was extraordinarily like many other communities in the region in which old commoner, or preexisting, groups had been eclipsed by young lineages of an expansive royal house. Mukama was a prince. Whatever the facts of his conception or the quality and meaning of his possession, Mukama Womunafu carried the status of *mulangira*, prince, and so did his sons. The legitimacy of this status appears never to have been challenged.

In Busoga, the statuses of prince and commoner were clearly differentiated. The primary demarcation was filiation, for the individual drew his or her status from the father. Beyond ascription, the meaning of the boundary between the two statuses was denoted in the patterns of deferential speech and behavior and in the differential routines of administrative and judicial decision making that had emerged by Womunafu's day.

The difference in status was not only well marked but also of extreme importance. The meaning and tension that ran through the relational networks joining, and separating, princes and commoners constituted the ultimate basis of a system of political domination. Such a play of status differentiation is observed right through the Lake Victoria region, though the details vary from place to place. On the western side of the region, such ideas of differentiated status touched, fixed, and occasionally closed boundaries between social groups, creating structures of a classlike or castelike character.

In precolonial Busoga, the coupling of ideas of prominence and prestige with an expansive royal patrilineage created a system of allocation of authority that could be sustained for many generations. In the nineteenth century, sharp and significant social differentiation between princes and commoners, based upon a conscious elaboration of prerogative, may be noted. What mattered at mid-century— just after 1855 in Luuka—was the capacity to deploy force, and here the princes were predominant. Even in relatively open states such as Luuka and Bugabula—where the granting of high-level authority to commoners was an important instrument of state expansion—few commoners managed to achieve levels of authority comparable to those of princes.

It is equally clear from the study of the case of Bunafu that the distinction between statuses, while clearly marked, was not *fixed*. Rather, it was a matter of considerable debate and conflict, and its precise character varied in time and from place to place. Wholesale changes in the character of relations between royal persons and commoners are observed in the nineteenth century with the execution of Kakuku in Buganda and again following the installation of Mudhungu and then again soon after the seating of Nabwana Inhensiko II.

The increase in princely prerogative in Luuka after 1855 was the consequence of a relatively simple, yet fundamental, change in structure. The old senior line—the narrow lineage of men prescribed to rule—had lost its capacity to sustain itself with the sudden death of Kakuku in Buganda. No longer would the capacity to rule be confined to the ruler's favorite son or sons. With the passage of authority outward from this small core of potential successors, the number of men with the "capacity" to succeed underwent

156

geometric expansion. There was a breach of the once well-articulated principle distinguishing the few princes eligible to rule and those clearly ineligible. More importantly, the boundary between a prominence ascribed and a prerogative demanded had been eroded.

The effects of this shift of attention of an elevated group from simply the maintenance of prominence toward the exercise of prerogative were felt place by place, settlement by settlement, over the whole of Luuka during the decade and a half from 1855. The effects were felt in the relational networks that enveloped the princes, in their capacities to divest old, nonroyal families of their estates, in the degree of day-to-day control they could exercise over their commoners, and in the volume of service princes felt due them by commoners. This was Luuka, and this was Bunafu. And this was Bugweri, Bukooli, Busiki, and Bulamogi, all states in Busoga in which such eras of princes occurred in the nineteenth century, raising the levels of tension between princes and commoners. Commoners with ancient credentials were either levered out of estates or left voluntarily. And while new commoner groups arrived amidst the eras of princes seeking new opportunities, they were without land and status, and therefore much weaker than the older groups, much less able to influence events through position and relationship, and therefore rather more inclined to use physical force.

It would be a mistake to see the extension and intensification of *royal domination* entailed in the eras of princes as synonymous with the growth of the state and of its center. Relations hardened during these periods not only between princes and commoners but also between the nodes of princely activity and the old political capitals. Eras of princes interrupted the flow of power to the center, slowed the development of the capital as a political and administrative center, reduced the scale of the political corporation,

157

drew into conflict the emerging trade networks and markets, and weakened the capacity of the larger society to respond to the new challenges of the late nineteenth century.

Amidst these reverberations, we may glimpse the emergence of a struggle occurring on a rather different plane. Beyond the conflicts over land and loyalty between royal men such as Womunafu and commoners such as Nafa and beyond the competition for centrality and legitimacy, which surfaced among princely outposts and old capitals, there was an ideological struggle. This struggle developed between individuals, lineages, and coalitions that appear to have been content with, or enthusiastic about, elevated princely prerogative after Kakuku's death, and other individuals and groups that wished to reconstruct Luuka, to revivify the political center, and to restrict the prerogatives of the princes. That Kabalu and her kin maintained such great influence over an eighty-year period suggests the importance of their alignment not just with an individual but with a complex of ideas of political rights voiced through the issue of filial succession. The sources are not rich enough to detail this ideological contest within the community, but they are sufficient to suggest that such a contest was experienced. In the movement to seat Mudhungu on the Luuka stool and in the premature seating of Nabwana Inhensiko II, one may be observing the faint lines of conscious policy.

What is illuminated in these several layers of conflict is that these political communities—the Luuka state and the Bunafu community—were constructed and reformed slowly through the play of several social institutions—marriage, kinship, elevated status, and clientship. These political communities were not simple conquest states carved out by roving bands of heavily armed young men acting in behalf of a prince. Forty years elapsed between the moment when the construction of Mukama's first enclosure began and the moment when the "conquest" of Nafa was finally effected.

158

Time, here, underlines the processual means by which
dominance was achieved and the "state" completed. It
suggests the significance of the *formed*, and not only the
given, components of authority.

Prince Womunafu as Mukama was also a figure of certain
exceptional attributes which extend his experience beyond
that of a prince on the frontier of a state. While in the experience of the prince one may note certain *formed* aspects
of authority, what is disclosed in the observation of the Mukama of the nineteenth century is authority in its *fixed* aspect. Mukama is, in this sense, a *formula* of authority as
well as a prince, headman, child, man, father, sibling, and
mate. Mukama was recognized at, or before birth, to have
certain qualities centering on possession by spirits, in particular a transcendent relationship with a heroic Mukama
considered parent of the royal dynasties of the region. Mukama, here, is an idea eternalized, reawakened occasionally
in the person of a prince, a lineage-oriented idea unencum-
bered by the orderly rules of succession and inheritance.
Around this center, the eternalized Mukama, one may perceive within the formula of Mukama several prominent
elements: the lingering appeal of ideas, institutions, and behavior borne by Lwo and once Lwo-speaking groups in
northern and central Busoga; a defensive interest in the representation of Nyoro hegemony in a region beyond the control of the rulers of the Bunyoro kingdom; the conservation
of a *valued* mobility; and an attachment to a concept of individual exalted status.

POSSESSION

In Busoga, there were no highly organized and well-regu-
lated spirit-possession cults such as have been identified in
the western areas of the Lake Victoria region. Yet spirit
possession formed a central part of the religious life of the
people of the Busoga region. It was not merely that the

159

world was composed of spirits as well as man but that these spirits had the capacity to communicate with and to act through and upon man. Certain people in the society were considered predisposed toward states of possession or were actually possessed. Within the royal families of northern and central Busoga, men who were so predisposed or possessed were called Mukama, for they were considered to be possessed or likely to be possessed by the spirit of the heroic Mukama who had once lived on the earth. As noted, a man so diagnosed as being possessed by Mukama was surrounded by specialists, some of whom themselves were possessed. That the most potent instances of possession should focus upon members of royal families brought within one general system ideas of superordination and ideas of possession of quite distinct origin. And while concepts of spirit power and ideas of possession were important throughout the societies of the Busoga area, the particular environment of the Mukama was one in which such ideas and practice were distinctively concentrated.

It is this concentration that constitutes the most general characteristic distinguishing the community of Bunafu from other communities in the region. Bunafu was a community of intensity. It was in Bunafu that kingly palaces were built for a village headman. It was in Bunafu that the guides of spirit possession congregated. It was at Bunafu that communication with a number of deities was sought, and it was within the orbit of the community that spirits themselves were sensed to congregate. A very old man in 1971 was able to recall a visit to Twesudde a few years after Mukama left that enclosure around 1887. He remembers above all else the restrictions imposed upon him there. "When somebody went out of his house at night, he would have to cover himself with a barkcloth, and if you failed to do so you would meet the leopard of the spirit who could maul you and eat you. And if you had to defecate or urinate you could not do it in the garden, but rather had to go very far away into the bush or the spirit Mukama would beat you."[1]

Lwo

Mukama Womunafu, like the heroic Mukama who is said to have crossed Busoga, was surrounded by an array of symbols that today are identified with the Lwo-speaking or once Lwo-speaking peoples of the wider region. Lwo speakers traveled into northern and central Busoga in the seventeenth and eighteenth centuries and settled among Bantu-speaking groups. From within these Lwo groups emerged the founding cores of the states of northern, central, and eastern Busoga, of the dynasties that would still be bearing power at the beginning of the twentieth century. Beyond Mukama Womunafu himself, descendants of early Lwo speakers in Busoga played roles of considerable importance in the early days of the Bukanga enclosure. And toward the end of the nineteenth century, the descendants of the Lwo-speaking migrants who had earlier reached this region of northern Luuka appear to have constituted a group of some conscious and corporate form (even after having ceased to speak Lwo), for their daughters were carefully avoided in the elaborate marriage networks that developed around Mukama at each enclosure. Mukama, as a formula, may have given new vitality to many old ideas of Lwo cast. At a minimum, Bunafu was an enclosed zone within which the integration of once Lwo-speaking groups into the surrounding society would be significantly delayed.

Nyoro

Bunafu lay some 150 kilometers beyond the closest lands over which the kings of Bunyoro exercised regular authority. Far removed, Nyoro influence was nevertheless significant. Traders associated with Nyoro markets and Nyoro centers of production brought valued Nyoro goods to locations within the range of Bunafu. (See map 17, chapter VII.) Pastoralists moved back and forth between Nyoro areas of present-day Buruli and Bugerere and the lands of northern Busoga. Migrants from the Bunyoro kingdom brought ideas of Nyoro cast and Nyoro ways of doing things to areas far beyond the frontiers of Nyoro authority. The representational idea—in Nyoro dress, in Soga place—was an instrument of antithesis within a world that was increasingly coming into the orbit of the kings of Buganda. In name and in style, Mukama evoked Bunyoro in Busoga.

This Nyoro idea was of such importance ideologically that the region of northern Busoga came to be known as "Bunyoro" in the discourse of people of southern Busoga at the turn of the century. The representational idea of Mukama, king of Bunyoro, must have been of particular relevance in the aftermath of such destructive pillaging as occurred over a great region of Busoga during the *ekyetoloolo* campaign. The Nyoro association could have served as a tool in the renovation of societies affected by that campaign. The evocation of Mukama affirmed that there was a great power in the region opposed to, at war with, Buganda. And it was in the aftermath of *ekyetoloolo,* at the moment when Kagoda and Wambuzi were attempting to reconstruct their kingdoms, that the great enclosure at Bukanga was built for the young Mukama of Busoga.

MOBILITY

The traditions of the heroic Mukama disclose a figure steadily on the move, building new enclosures for himself and his followers, drawing in clients along the way, leaving behind wives and children, moving, eventually, beyond the region across which communication among members of a common ancestry was possible. In this *progress*, Mukama only involves himself in the quintessential aspects of a ruler's life—the enlistment of support, the recruitment of wives, the fathering of men, and the erection of monumental enclosures. The ideal of the pastoralist, or hunter, or migrant is maintained. There is no compromise with permanent settlement. There is no notion of establishing rights in the soil through long-term occupation. The progress is a passage of inherent authority, which requires no landed legitimation. It is a passage that finds its momentum in the acquisition of supporters, not land; in the creation of centers, not estates; in the establishment of cores, not administrations.

In Bunafu, as noted, the idea of mobility is counterpoised to that of settlement. Mukama had to move to maintain the character of his prestige. Mukama had to draw new support along the way rather than depend upon the old. Mukama had to leave behind wives, sons, enclosures, in order to survive. New cores worked, administration did not. This idea of valued mobility was given life in Mukama at a time when large numbers of people in the region were on the move, or ready to move, to seek new opportunities elsewhere. It was at Bunafu that mobility, as a value, was dramatized. And it was there that the mobility of the ancient and heroic Mukama measurable in kilometers was reenacted in measures of meters.

EXALTED STATUS

Within the experience of Mukama, an idea of individual exalted status was actualized. Mukama, possessed, was raised to an exalted status not shared by most of his royal kinsmen. Here, this idea of an individualized status is opposed to the idea of the exalted status of a collateral agnatic group—the royal house, the *balangira* or *karuoth*.[2]

163

Through the principle of the *karuoth* alone, authority could not collect at a particular point or in the person of an individual member of the collateral group. Rather, prestige and dominance diffused outward to younger and newer members of the exalted group. It is the emergence of the lineage of the heroic Mukama in the eastern and later central and northern regions of Busoga that provides one of the first glimpses of narrowed lines of authority in the region between the Nile and the Mpologoma.³ The individual exalted status was in turn passed to sons of the heroic Mukama and to others who successfully claimed association with the lineage of the heroic Mukama and who were thereby seated as rulers of the various states in the north. But this individual status was also available to selected princes of the royal houses who were not ruling and would never rule, being accorded to individuals such as the son of Mukanni through the diagnosis of possession. While Mukama, unlike the king, could not pass on his individual status to a son or brother, he did command, at certain points in his lifetime, legitimate power of a kind similar to that of kings. *Mukama* and *king*, descendant from the same complex of ideas of a heroic Mukama, were the two preeminent roles in the society, each radiating forward from node to node and generation to generation ideas of authority, dominance, and status.

These five elements of this formula of authority are discussed here in their *static* aspect. But one might ask: what is the structural play of such a formula over time? In respect to Mukama Womunafu, the formula of authority was invested with life within the child of Mukanni at a moment of general crisis, found its context on the margins of a state, and secured its adherents among a collection of mobile individuals and groups seeking security. As a child, Mukama functioned as the focal point of an entirely new community, of a pattern of recruitment, of a system of labor obligation, and of a network of social linkage.

Viewed as a formula of authority, Mukama appears less able to sustain its substructure of ideas, undergoing occasional revivification with the erection of new enclosures and the enlistment of new support, but in time more deeply influenced by other ideas of authority and other patterns of political action. It was, indeed, a formula of authority that seems to have passed through its mature phase while Mukama was but a child. In this mature phase, Mukama joined within one complex a system of thought and explanation and a pattern of action parallel to, and separate from, that of the state. But later, beyond its mature phase, Mukama was incapable of arresting the ambitions of the princes; was unable to sustain the ideals of Lwo life as sons were raised among groups that had never been Lwo speaking; failed to produce the power of the Bunyoro kingdom on the soil of Busoga; could not maintain the heightened value of mobility, each new enclosure becoming less significant than the one before; and could not engender a concept of individual exalted status conveyable to the next generation.

Over time, the authority of Mukama in its formulaic aspect was increasingly penetrated by the network of ideas and behavior radiating from the political capitals. Bunafu, consequently, became, at one time, more like, and more part of, Luuka society. The generative capacity of a new center of authority, Bunafu, drawing forward and radiating outward ideas of the ancient and heroic Mukama, was arrested by the forces of the conventional world. The enclosure was breached. The eternalized Mukama would unveil himself elsewhere at some future time.

Appendix: The Construction
of a Chronology

THE traditions utilized in the reconstruction of Bunafu's past emit a variety of temporal characteristics. There are references of a *perpetual* nature—"the burial of the chiefs would last eight days"; "the Bakyega were the pot makers." There are countless statements of a *sequential* character—"the son of Kidolo was Kitubi"; "Kidolo was living when Womunafu first came to Bunafu." Some statements are quite explicit in presenting a temporal context yet *general* in actual reference—"during the reign of Wambuzi"; "during the life of Bakungaine"; "before the famine of Kyasanga"; "around the time of the *ekyetoloolo* campaign." Still other statements are both explicit in terms of temporal context and *specific* in terms of moment, though not indicating an exact date—"Waidhuuba Mulawa was killed with his master Kakuku in the time of Suna"; "Bwenene was taken from Bwebya by Baganda returning from installing Miro."

The identification of these four general categories of temporal references in the collected traditions is a beginning. But the traditions containing evidence on the precolonial past of the Lake Victoria region provide no dates. Here the historian is presented with a problem of no small dimension. Change in the past cannot be comprehended without reference to chronology. Even where a general sort of periodization is educed from tradition (in terms of the reigns of a dynasty of kings or in terms of "before" or "after" some notable event), the situation of the historian is hardly comfortable. Such generality in reckoning time in the past confounds the analysis of change. It masks the possible relationship among overtly remote phenomena. It masks short-

166

run change that occurs within a reign. It masks linkages among events in several regions.

For the historian interested in change in the short run and in the relatedness of several events, the necessary tasks are obvious. First, there is the need to make more finite the temporal divisions educed from tradition. Here the introduction of a larger body of evidence on a greater number of events (whether important or unimportant) may establish a tighter sequence, interposing secondary and tertiary temporal boundaries between the more distant boundaries of the "traditional" periods. (See figure 8.) Second, there is the

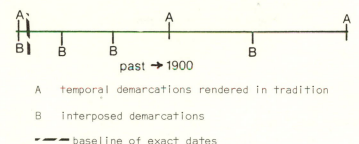

A   temporal demarcations rendered in tradition

B   interposed demarcations

━ ━ ━ baseline of exact dates

FIGURE 8 ● Chronology: First Stage

need to link events directly or indirectly to known or credibly estimated dates. Travelers may record the names of living rulers or, as did Stanley,[1] the alleged age of accession of the reigning monarch and the length of reign of his predecessor. Tradition may record the visit of a traveler at a particular moment in a ruler's career, possibly datable phenomena such as eclipses or droughts, or the length of a reign. Archaeological evidence may provide relative dating of periods of occupation of capital sites or of the introduction of certain kinds of trade goods that are linked through tradition to a particular reign. (See figure 9.) Third, there is the need to extend the firmer and more finite chronology to

167

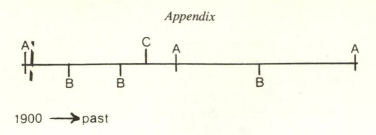

1900 ⟶ past

A temporal demarcations rendered in tradition

B interposed demarcations

C known date in past

▬▬◂ baseline of exact dates

FIGURE 9 ● Chronology: Second Stage

processes, events, and persons that do not announce their own chronology. Here one may be able to identify a set of synchronisms or "tie-ins" that relate events in one area for which a chronological sequence is poorly revealed to ones for which a chronology (in part at least) is more certain—to bring within the compass of firmer chronology events occurring over a very wide area. (See figure 10.) Fourth, there is the need to establish a firmer and deeper baseline in the past from which less conjectural extrapolations of chronology in the deeper past may be executed. (See figure 11.)

The construction of a chronology of Bunafu's past has involved the use of all four of these modes of calculation of time in the past in the analysis of a series of crucial or central "events." The evidential base encompasses not only the records or reconstructions of these events, but also *five* sequential frameworks, and a mass of related data.

168

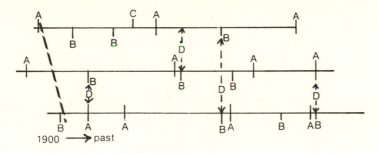

A   temporal demarcations rendered in tradition

B   interposed demarcations

C   known date in past

D   synchronism or "tie-in"

—— baseline of exact dates

FIGURE 10 • Chronology: Third Stage

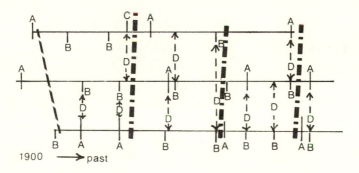

A   temporal demarcations rendered in tradition

B   interposed demarcations

C   known date in past

D   synchronism or "tie-in"

——. baseline of exact dates

▪▪▪▪ baseline of estimated dates

FIGURE 11 • Chronology: Fourth Stage

THE SEQUENTIAL FRAMEWORKS

The Sequence of Sites Occupied by Mukama Womunafu

The series encompasses: a. "before the Makutu camp"
b. "before Bukanga"
c. enclosure 1 (Bukanga)
d. enclosure 2 (Twesudde)
e. enclosure 3 (Bwebya)
f. enclosure 4 (Buganda)
g. "after Mukama's death in 1906"

Directly or indirectly, points in the careers of hundreds of men and women can be related to one or another of these periods. Periods c, d, and e are further defined by the sequences of births of male children (who survived to maturity) in each enclosure.

The Dynastic Genealogy of Luuka

The series encompasses: a. "before Nhiro"
b. Nhiro
c. Inhensiko I
d. Wambuzi
e. Kakuku   f. Kalogo   g. Kibalya
h. Mudhungu
i. Inhensiko II, died in 1920

Again, the careers of hundreds of men and women can be related to one or another of these reign periods either directly or indirectly. There is also a recollected series of wars with Buganda and neighboring countries, which provides an "interior" sequence. Likewise, the births of the surviving sons of the rulers and their careers provide a sequence that further defines the reigns of the Luuka rulers.

The Dynastic Genealogy of Buganda from the Reign of Juko to the Beginning of the Reign of Mwanga in 1884[2]

The series encompasses:

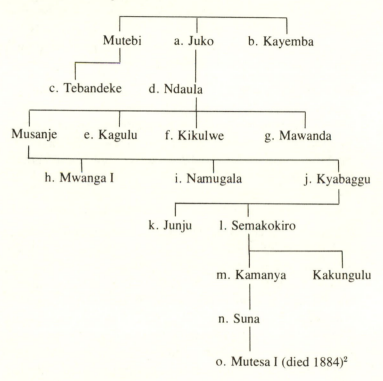

[Note: Musanje and Kakungulu did not rule]

In the dynastic genealogies of Buganda, Kabaka Juko is noted as belonging to the twelfth or thirteenth generation. Most of the rulers from Mawanda forward to Mutesa were involved in events in the Busoga region, and some of the rulers of Buganda are linked directly or indirectly to events within the Luuka kingdom.

Appendix

The Capitals of Buganda Occupied
by Kabaka Suna II and by Kabaka Mutesa I

The series encompasses:
a. Mulago	g. Kabojja
b. Nabulagala	h. Lubaga
c. Nakatema	i. Kikwandwa
d. Bbanda	j. Lubaga
e. Nakawa	k. Nabulagala
f. Nabulagala	

Some of these capitals were visited by people from the Busoga area providing more precise indications of temporal context. Some were visited by people from outside the Lake Victoria region, and the time of occupation of a particular capital by the Kabaka was noted in the contemporary sources.

A Series of Generations of Averaged Length

Historians of precolonial Africa have applied notional averages to generation lengths in estimating elapsed time in the past. This tool has been used in two ways. First, it has been used to estimate time in the past on the basis of a line of descent, counting the generation as the period from the birth of a man to the time of the birth of his first son, multiplying the notional average times the number of intervening generations. Second, it has been used to estimate time in the past on the basis of a sequence of rulers in a dynasty, using a similar estimate of average reign length (from the time of accession of one ruler to the time of succession of his first succeeding son of the next generation). Calculations based on notional averages of reign lengths tend to be quite imperfect, given the problem of establishing a sound estimate of an average, the problem of determining an average applicable to several lineages, and the problem of complex succession patterns (fraternal and collateral rather than filial).

172

Moreover, there is the fundamental problem of establishing the identity of the senior son in each generation, to prevent distortion due to the tendency of successions to drift toward junior members of each generation. Yet where one is confident of the genealogical constructions and where one uses the notional average generation length in conjunction with harder evidence, the tool can be quite helpful in filling gaps between lineages of secondary importance and the series that constitutes the four sequential frameworks discussed above. The notional average generation can also be used cautiously in extending backward the firmer chronologies.[3]

THE TIMING OF THE CENTRAL EVENTS

Twelve events have been identified that are fundamental to the construction of a chronology of Bunafu's past. They are:

1. Mukama Womunafu's evacuation of Bwebya enclosure and his removal to the new Buganda enclosure
2. Mukama Womunafu's evacuation of Twesudde enclosure and the move to the new enclosure at Bwebya
3. The installation of Inhensiko II as ruler of Luuka
4. The appointment of Bawalamayi as *kitwikiro* of Mukama Womunafu
5. The eclipse of Nafa
6. The installation of Mudhungu as ruler of Luuka
7. Kakuku's execution in Buganda
8. The emigration of Wagubona and Lubagu and sons from Bunafu to Bugabula
9. The death of Wambuzi and accession of his son Kakuku
10. The erection of the enclosure at Bukanga
11. The sacking of Monkey clan settlements in Bulondoganyi and the migration of Chuka and his son Wagubona to Luuka
12. The arrival of Nafa in the lands north of the Nabisira

An attempt has been made to establish a fixed date for each of these events. The processes of deduction are recapitulated below.

Mukama Womunafu's Evacuation of Bwebya Enclosure and His Removal to the New Buganda Enclosure: 1892

Mukama Womunafu left Bwebya shortly after his daughter Bwenene was kidnapped from the enclosure by Baganda passing through the area. The sources place this incident at the time of the installation of Miro as ruler of the Kigulu state (to the east of Luuka). Miro was installed through the intervention of a Ganda army accompanied by Captain F. Lugard in 1892. This may be taken as the point of commencement of the colonial period in Busoga.

Mukama Womunafu's Evacuation of Twesudde Enclosure and the Move to the New Enclosure at Bwebya: 1887±2

The evacuation of Twesudde occurred at least several years after the installation of Inhensiko II as ruler of Luuka (1878±1). Sources relate that Mukama Womunafu occupied the Bwebya enclosure for no more than five years, meaning approximately 1887 to 1892. Mukama was still occupying Twesudde when Muziramulungi was appointed *kitwikiro* of Luuka by Inhensiko II ca. 1884.

The Installation of Inhensiko II as Ruler of Luuka: 1878±1

According to Kaggwa, the campaign that took Wambuzi to Mawembe and plundered Kalimugi occurred while Kabaka Mutesa was at Lubaga and just before the arrival of Lieutenant Smith and Reverend C. T. Wilson at Lubaga on June 30, 1877. The Ganda campaign was led by the Musoga Balikumbuga who had been made a *kitongole* chief in Buganda.[4] Kalimugi here is, of course, the ruler of Luuka at the time, Mudhungu Kalimwigi. Wambuzi is Wambuzi Kyobe, the dissident prince challenging Mudhungu's authority. In the campaign Mudhungu's palace was burned, and Mudhungu was seriously wounded by a spear. Inhensiko II was brought from Bulamogi and was installed as ruler. He took the throne while Mudhungu was still alive. In fact, Mudhungu lived on for about two more years in a separate palace. Inhensiko's first act was to gather a small army and to wipe out Wambuzi Kyobe and his supporters living in the area of Mawembe Hill.

The Appointment of Bawalamayi as Kitwikiro of Mukama Womunafu: 1870s

Bawalamayi was appointed *kitwikiro* after Nagaya (of the same clan) had been appointed chief of the Nawansega division of Luuka by Mudhungu. Inhensiko II replaced Nagaya with Naluwairo, of the Mabiro clan, in the first few years of his reign. Since it is unlikely that Mukama Womunafu would have appointed Bawalamayi as *kitwikiro* after Nagaya had been dismissed, one may assume that Bawalamayi was appointed during Mudhungu's reign, or in the 1870s. We also know that Bawalamayi had served as *kitwikiro* for some years before Mukama Womunafu left Twesudde and moved to Bwebya (1887±2).

The Eclipse of Nafa: ca. 1870

This was, of course, not an event definable in terms of a specific moment. But an approximate 1870 date for the completion of the process of destruction of Nafa's power is derived from the timing of the migration of members of Nafa's own lineage from Bunafu to Bugabula. Most of those who are recalled as having left Bunafu traveled west to Bugabula arriving there in the reign of Kitamirike I, Gabula Namugweri. Kitamirike ruled for several years after Kabaka Suna's death (ca. 1856), and Kitamirike succeeded his father, Kagoda, who had died a few years after Suna had been installed as ruler of Buganda. On this basis,

Kitamirike ruled from 1840±5 to 1863±4. It is likely that the kin of Nafa who escaped Bunafu reached Bugabula in the last years of Kitamirike's reign. They almost certainly would have been too young to make the journey in the earlier years.

A second way of reckoning the timing of the migration of Nafa's kin to Bugabula is based on the assumption that they left the Bunafu area only after the erection of Mukama Womunafu's Twesudde enclosure ca. 1860. Twesudde was erected around the time of the death of the ruler of Luuka named Kalogo. Kakuku, Kalogo's predecessor, had been executed in Buganda (1855±3) in the last year or two of Kabaka Suna's reign. Tradition records that Kalogo ruled only for a year or so. By this reasoning, Twesudde was built in 1857±5. The emigration of Nafa's kin then may be estimated to have taken place between 1857±5 and 1863±4, when Kitamirike of Bugabula died. The underlying assumption throughout this analysis is that the emigration of Nafa's kin signaled the end of Nafa's authority in the area.

The Installation of Mudhungu as Ruler of Luuka: 1870

Various sources relate that Mudhungu was installed as ruler of Luuka immediately after word was received of the execution of his father, Kakuku, in Buganda (1855±3). If this were true, he did not exercise his role until later and stayed throughout the following years outside of Luuka, lodged in the capital of the ruler of Bugabula, Kitamirike I, Gabula Namugweri. The big chiefs that might have supported his succession were killed with Kakuku, and only slowly over a number of years did sufficient support coalesce to bring about (with Ganda assistance) the overthrow of Kibalya, who himself had overthrown Kalogo. The death of Kibalya is taken here as the beginning of Mudhungu's reign.

The overthrow of Kibalya was accomplished with the assistance of a Ganda army led by Mmandwambi, the

Ssekiboobo of Kyaggwe, sent by Kabaka Mutesa to install Mudhungu. Kaggwa places this campaign during the period when Mutesa was at his capital at Nabulagala between the visit of Speke and Grant and the visit of Stanley.[5] Mutesa occupied Nabulagala from 1868 or 1869 until about 1872, and the Mmandwambi campaign is placed within these dates. Kaggwa further records that this campaign against Kibalya took place after Mutesa's third Ramadhan fast in 1869 and before his fourth Ramadhan in November-December 1870.[6]

Kakuku's Execution in Buganda: 1855 ±3

Kaggwa's recounting of the reign of Suna does not mention Kakuku by name. However, Kaggwa mentions at least two occasions upon which Basoga were executed in Buganda and a third upon which Basoga were massacred for having "rebelled again because of Suna's wanton execution of all their chiefs."[7] Kaggwa places these events close to the end of Suna's reign (ca. 1856). These executions appear to have occurred after the 1852 visit of an Arab trader to Suna's court (described to Richard Burton in 1857)[8] and before the visit of Speke to the Kabaka's court, which occurred during the reign of Suna's successor Mutesa in 1862.[9] By 1862 not only had Kakuku been executed, but Kalogo had ruled for about a year and been killed, the woman Kabalu had been plundered by a deputy of Mutesa, and Kibalya had been ruling for at least two years, giving an early date of 1852 and a late date of 1858-59 for the execution of Kakuku.

It would be helpful here to have a more certain date for Suna's death. Stanley, writing in 1878, and basing his remarks on his observations in Buganda in 1875-76, remarks, "when we come to Suna II, the son of Kamanya, and predecessor and father of Mtesa [Mutesa], we are told that he was about sixteen years of age when he succeeded to his father, and about forty when he died, and that he reigned, therefore, twenty-four years. As Mtesa ascended the throne in his nineteenth year, and as he has already reigned fifteen years [up to 1875] Suna must have been born in 1820, begun to reign in 1836, and died in 1860."[10] But J. M. Gray has argued rather persuasively for a date of 1856 as the time of Suna's death and the seating of Mutesa.[11]

The Emigration of Wagubona and Lubagu and Sons from Bunafu to Bugabula: 1850s

Soon after they reached Bugabula, Mulondo and Isakwa—sons of Wagubona and Lubagu—were given *mitala* and *bisoko* offices by Kitamirike I, Gabula Namugweri, who ruled Bugabula from 1840±5 to 1863±4. Presumably Mulondo and Isakwa were mature men (between the ages, say, of 20 and 40) when they left Bunafu, and this would correlate with the estimated date for Wagubona's departure from Bulondoganyi: early 1800s.

Employing the notional average of twenty-seven years per generation, the estimated date of Isakwa's birth would be 1819 and that of his eldest brother Mulondo would be 1815.

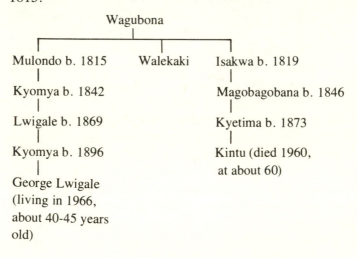

These estimated dates would have Mulondo and Isakwa as mature men in the time of Kitamirike I, Gabula Namugweri. It is difficult to establish any more definite timing except to remark that they would have been too young to reap the rich rewards in Bugabula had they migrated from Bunafu during the first half of Kitamirike's reign. This is why the migration is placed in the 1850s. A more accurate dating does not appear to be required by the argument in the body of the present work.

The Death of Wambuzi and Accession of His Son Kakuku: ca. 1841

Wambuzi died some years after the *ekyetoloolo* campaign (ca. 1830), for traditions suggest that he contributed considerable energy and time to the reconstruction of the kingdom after the Ganda campaign. While tradition has Wambuzi as a contemporary of Kabaka Kamanya, we know that he was still ruling Luuka in the early years of Suna's reign. Stanley provided 1836 for the commencement of Suna's reign.[12]

Wambuzi died before his neighbor Kagoda of Bugabula, for Kakuku had dealings with both Kagoda and his successor Kitamirike I. Kagoda appears to have died in the middle years of Suna's reign, before the execution of Wangobo, ruler of Bugweri, by a Ganda force. People fled Bugweri at that time, carrying with them accounts of the pillaging of Wangobo, and found Kitamirike I ruling Bugabula when they arrived there. Kagoda died then in 1846±5.

These few fragmentary pieces of evidence provide outside limits of 1836 and 1846±5 for the timing of the death of Wambuzi, and here a rough middle ground of ca. 1841 is taken as the time of transfer of power from Wambuzi to Kakuku. It is unlikely that Kakuku began to rule much after 1841, for his son Mudhungu was born in his palace and is said to have been mature by the time his father was executed (1855±3). After all, Mudhungu had a son, Inhensiko II, who was already going to war in 1877. If Inhensiko II were born in 1856 or 1857 or 1858 as is variously alleged (and this would make him a young man of about twenty at the time of his accession to the kingship of Luuka), Mudhungu could hardly have been born later than 1841.

The Erection of the Enclosure at Bukanga: ca. 1830

Tradition indicates that Mukama Womunafu was about ten years old when the enclosure was built at Bukanga. Tradition indicates that the erection of the enclosure came after the *ekyetoloolo* campaign. Tradition relates that Wambuzi was ruling Luuka when the enclosure was built. Tradition indicates indirectly that Kamanya was ruling Buganda at the time of the erection of the first enclosure at Bunafu.

Stanley suggested that Suna's reign began in 1836, thus that Kamanya's ended at that time. Kaggwa records that the *ekyetoloolo* campaign was undertaken while Kamanya was staying at his capital at Mpumudde, which was the eighth of eleven occupations of the some ten capital sites mentioned by Kaggwa.[13] One could speculate on this simple basis that Mpumudde and therefore *ekyetoloolo* belong to the later years of Kamanya's reign. Kaggwa relates, however, that following the *ekyetoloolo* campaign and one other, there was "an interval of many peaceful years."[14] If, with this remark in mind, one moves the *ekyetoloolo* campaign back to the middle of Kamanya's reign, takes the Stanley estimate of 1836 for the close of Kamanya's life, and takes a notional twenty-seven years for Kamanya's reign, a date of 1822-1823 would be suggested.

In chapter III, it was suggested that the *ekyetoloolo* campaign came during a period of extended drought and food shortages, which made necessary the organization of a foraging campaign to the east and made possible the movement of large armies through and across what in normal years would be great expanses of river and swamp. Survey-

ing Kaggwa's narration of the campaigns of Kamanya
around the time of *ekyetoloolo*, one notes a considerable
number of campaigns on the northern and northeastern margins of Buganda, considerable unrest among nominally
Ganda communities in these areas, and heightened conflict
between Ganda and Nyoro armies along this same frontier.
One of the objects of the campaigns of Kamanya to the
northeast was to still the incursions and raids of peoples
from the north of Lake Kyoga to the lands to the south
—Bugerere, Buruli, and Bulemezi. Twentieth-century
droughts in Uganda tend to develop out of the movement
from northeast to southwest of the boundaries of rainfall
sufficiency. Cattle keepers in the drier lands to the northeast
press south and southwest in search of securer sources of
water and foodstuffs. Marginal and settled agriculturalists
look to the moister lands to the south and southwest in and
across the Lake Kyoga basin. Could this sort of shunting of
quite desperate groups of migrants have been the essential
problem along the northeast frontier of Buganda in Kamanya's day? There is no explicit tradition from Buganda
indicating a period of famine, and drought may not have actually struck the core lands of the Buganda state. But the
campaign of *ekyetoloolo* in Busoga looks very much like a
foraging expedition.

There is substantial evidence of extended and significant
drought and famine in northeast and eastern Africa some
time in the 1820s and 1830s, a "Great Famine" of the region. There are indications of famine in this time in contemporary written sources and in traditions. The present
writer has considered elsewhere the possibility of using the
minimum readings of the Nile Flood at the Roda Gauge in
the Nile Delta as a means of estimating upward and downward trends in the levels of the lakes of the East African region and from there the upward and downward trends in
precipitation levels in the Lake region.[15] A tentative esti-

mate from these calculations places a drought about 1833, or slightly earlier.

The reckoning of the timing of the erection of the enclosure at Bukanga would then focus on the period between the crudely estimated date of 1822 for the mid-point of Kamanya's reign to about 1836, when Kamanya's reign closed, according to Stanley. One cannot get closer to an exact date without fixing more firmly the date of the *ekyetoloolo* campaign and without establishing the precise temporal relationship of the *ekyetoloolo* campaign to the erection of the enclosure at Bukanga. A date of ca. 1830 is proposed.

The Sacking of Monkey Clan Settlements in Bulondoganyi and the Migration of Chuka and His Son Wagubona to Luuka: Early 1800s

Kaggwa relates that dissident Prince Kakungulu "invaded Bulondoganyi and killed Majwala, the Mulondo, with all his sub-chiefs."[16] This is almost certainly the sacking of Mulondo settlements which sent Chuka and Wagubona (of a Mulondo lineage) flying eastward, but Soga sources attribute the sacking not to the dissident prince but to Kamanya, the ruler of Buganda. Since Bulondoganyi was a battle-ground for both sides over a considerable period, the Mulondo communities may have actually been suffering from attacks from both sides.

The Kaggwa narrative places the Mulondo sacking early in Kamanya's reign, while Kamanya was residing in the third of eleven occupations of the some ten capital sites mentioned by the author.[17] When Chuka and Wagubona arrived in Luuka, they found Inhensiko I ruling the country. And Wagubona left the first settlement in Luuka for the lands north of the Nabisira while Inhensiko I was still ruling. Since Wambuzi had already been ruling Luuka for some years before the *ekyetoloolo* campaign, it is probable that the Mulondo sacking occurred five to fifteen years before *ekyetoloolo*. The sequence of events here would be:

a. Kamanya accedes to throne of Buganda.
b. The Mulondo sacking.
c. Chuka and Wagubona settle in southern Luuka during Inhensiko I's reign.
d. Wagubona leaves Luuka proper for the lands north of the Nabisira and marries Lubagu, daughter of Nafa.
e. Wambuzi succeeds his father Inhensiko I.
f. Some years later Luuka experiences the *ekyetoloolo* campaign.
g. The Bukanga enclosure is built for young Mukama during Wambuzi's reign (ca. 1830).
h. Kamanya dies and is succeeded by Suna (ca. 1836).
i. Wambuzi dies and is succeeded by Kakuku (ca. 1841).
j. Mudhungu is born.

There is other evidence on the timing of the sacking of Chuka and Wagubona. While less definitive, it is still of interest. Chuka's father was named Waluganja. Waluganja's father visited the palace of Kabaka Mawanda of Buganda. Oliver has estimated the reign of Mawanda as falling within the period 1717-44±38 years.[18] The present writer has elsewhere estimated the reign of Mawanda as falling into the period 1720-1747±32.[19] Kiwanuka has proposed 1734 as a probable date of death for Mawanda. The last estimate is based simply on an estimated reign generation—from death of last ruler of one generation to death of last ruler of subsequent generation—of thirty years. The first two estimates are based on a combination of an average reign generation of twenty-seven years and the postulated date of 1680 for an eclipse allegedly sighted in Buganda during the reign of Juko—two generations earlier than Mawanda's.[20]

If twenty-seven years is taken as a notional average generation length for the lineage of Wagubona, if the visit of Waluganja's father to the palace of Mawanda is fixed in the middle of Mawanda's reign (1734±32), and if the further assumption can be made that Waluganja's father was a mature man when he visited the palace, it is possible to compose a rough chronology for the lineage of Wagubona. This can in turn be compared to estimates of temporal contexts involving members of Wagubona's lineage derived from other modes of calculation. (See figure 12.)

Waluganja's father was a mature man in 1734±32
|
Waluganja was a mature man in 1761±32
|
Chuka was a mature man in 1788±32
|
Wagubona was a mature man in 1815±32[a]
|
Isakwa was a mature man in 1842±32[b]
|
Magobagobana was a mature man in 1869±32
|
Kyetima was a mature man in 1896±32
|
Kintu was a mature man in 1923±32[c]

[a] Wagubona reached Nafa's lands before *ekyetoloolo* (ca. 1830).
[b] Isakwa was given office by Kitamirike I of Bugabula who ruled 1840±5 to 1863±4.
[c] Kintu was twenty-three years old in 1923.

FIGURE 12 ● Chronology for Wagubona's Lineage

Even abandoning the margins of error, the simple estimates of timing of the age of maturity of the members of Wagubona's lineage based on the supposition of average generation, the crude estimate of the mid-point of Mawanda's reign, and the conjecture of Waluganja's father's age at the time of the visit to the palace of Mawanda, evoke an uncanny concordance with estimates of timing of activities of members of the lineage that have been arrived at independently.

The Arrival of Nafa in the Lands North of the Nabisira: Last Quarter of the Eighteenth Century

Traditions indicate that Nafa left his home in Bukono and traveled to the lands north of the Nabisira one or two generations before the arrival there of Wagubona and the marriage between Lubagu and Wagubona. The following sequence is observed:

a. arrival of Nafa
b. marriage of Nafa's son
c. birth of Lubagu
d. arrival of Wagubona north of the Nabisira
e. marriage of Wagubona and Lubagu
f. Wambuzi succeeds Inhensiko I
g. *ekyetoloolo*
h. erection of Bukanga enclosure (ca. 1830)

Such a sequence would seem to place the arrival of Nafa in Bunafu in the late eighteenth century.

There is no evidence available on the context of Nafa's departure from Bukono, but there is evidence of numerous emigrations from Bukono during the disastrous wars with Busiki, which occurred during the reigns of Kisozi and Ntumba Bukono and Mumesula and Muinda of Busiki. The outcome of these wars was that by the close of Muinda's reign the area under the control of the Busiki rulers had grown at the expense of Bukono. Tradition suggests that Muinda had a long reign. He died, indirect evidence indicates, during the early part of Kamanya's reign; that is, during the early part of the nineteenth century. If the departure of Nafa from Bukono is attributable to the losses sustained by Bukono during the wars with Busiki, the departure would have been in the late eighteenth century.

These twelve central events, their dating reckoned to different degrees of exactitude, constitute a chronological framework for the reconstruction of Bunafu's past, a framework that is used to establish the "moment" of various people and of a considerable number of events over a very large area.

Notes

Short titles are used below, the full references provided in the bibliography. The following abbreviations are used in the notes.

CTBTH   "Collected Texts: Busoga Traditional History," recorded in 1966-67 and in 1971-72. Original transcripts in possession of author.

STBTH   *Selected Texts: Busoga Traditional History*, xeroxed and bound edition of texts in three volumes, deposited in major Africana libraries and circulated by the author.

VS   Village survey of lower-level office holders in late nineteenth and early twentieth centuries in northern and central Busoga. The survey was begun in 1971 and was completed in 1973 and covers approximately 80 percent of the subcounties in the region, which today includes the former states of Bugabula, Buzaaya, Luuka, Bulamogi, Buzimba-Kigulu, Bugweri, Bukono, Busiki, and Bukooli. It provides a record of both office holders at the *mutala* (village) and *kisoko* (subvillage) levels and the constituencies of these officials in terms of clan and lineage affiliation.

INTRODUCTION

1. CTBTH, Text 542.

2. In CTBTH, more than 7,000 migrations are noted for the period from approximately 1700 to 1890. From around the middle of the eighteenth century through the fourth decade of the nineteenth century, an eastward pattern of emigration from the

Buganda region is evoked in the records of Busoga. It was not until the early nineteenth century, however, that a considerable northward flow of migrants from southern Busoga and the Lake Victoria littoral into the central and northern areas of Busoga is revealed in the collected traditions. An observed migrational trend from northeastern and eastern Busoga toward Bugabula in the second half of the nineteenth century is discussed in chapter VI.

3. This remarkable phrase of Hugh Trevor-Roper (*The Rise of Christian Europe*, p. 9) has been widely noted by African historians interested in overthrowing old and obviously deeply entrenched misconceptions of Africa and its past. The emerging picture of high rates of geographical mobility in precolonial eastern and central Africa must, over the next few years, generate new understandings of the development and operation of social and political institutions in the region. Analyses to date have been based largely on the premise of stable and quiescent populations.

4. Nonetheless, clan identity did have significance in a certain arena: marriage, the maintenance of tradition, and the coordination and alliance of related patrilineages living within one political unit. Lubagu and her father Nafa were of the Muganza clan, and Wagubona was of the Mulondo clan. These were but two of the some 240 patriclans found in Busoga in 1966.

5. CTBTH, Text 540.

6. In a long treatise—*Oral Tradition*—Jan Vansina stressed "the special nature of oral tradition" as a "chain of testimonies" (p. 46). He commented that a "proto-testimony of a tradition may undergo certain distortions during the course of transmission which are specifically due to the very process of transmission" (p. 45). While Vansina gave consideration in his study to informal texts and more open modes of transmission, his emphases— chains, the concept of proto-testimony, and the question of extent of distortion of the proto-testimony—were upon the more fixed forms of tradition and the narrow and closed modes of transmission. Recently, Vansina has revised his terms of reference and his argument (in "Once Upon a Time"), but the emphasis remains on

formal tradition and on framed modes of transmission. This approach gives little attention to the general processes of circulation of historical information in society which are not orderly, are not predictable, and are not reconstructable. In this sense, there is no "original tradition" and no discernible "chain of witnesses." While Vansina sees the "original tradition" and the "initial testimony" undergoing distortion through time until they are finally recorded by the historian as a historical testimony, this writer sees the historical testimony as the *outcome* of a variety of processes that essentially constitute the modes of communication of information in the society. The "historical memory" is not taken here to be a specialized "relay" either in content or mode of transmission.

7. CTBTH, Text 374.

8. The popular traditions of Mukama are considered at length in D. W. Cohen, *Historical Tradition*, chapters vi–ix.

CHAPTER I: THE BIRTH OF WOMUNAFU

1. CTBTH, Texts 559–561, 901, 918, and 930.

2. CTBTH, Texts 583, 935, and 937.

3. This speculative reconstruction is based on data from a great number of sources which indicate, variously, that Wambuzi's mother was Kabalu, that Inhensiko I's reign was exceedingly long, that Wambuzi was among the elder sons of Inhensiko, that Wambuzi was raised and stayed at Nsambya, that some of Wambuzi's brothers were disciplined by commoner chiefs, that Wambuzi was close to the Muluuta chief at Nasumiti at several points during his career, and that Wambuzi's installation was not accompanied by civil war.

4. See discussion of the Igobe lineage in Bunafu in chapter II.

5. CTBTH, Texts 915, 926, and 954. "Mukanni," interestingly, means "whose wife?" and denotes a woman who has had a child out of wedlock and whose child takes the lineage of the alleged father—with an emphasis on the public nature of illegitimacy. Of course, it is also a name given to girls so as to remember their antecedents who were called "Mukanni." Wambuzi's woman

was also called "Naigobe." It should be noted, as an aside, that while the legitimacy of various public figures in the nineteenth and twentieth centuries is a common subject of discussion and debate in Busoga today, the present writer heard no comment alleging that Wambuzi was not the one responsible for Mukanni's pregnancy.

6. The expansion of Lwo speakers over this enormous region is sketched out in Cohen, "The River-Lake Nilotes," pp. 135–149.

7. The inherent conflict within ruling houses in the region is more fully discussed in chapters V and VII. The problem of conflict within African royal families is given considerable attention in A. Southall, *Alur Society*; L. A. Fallers, *Bantu Bureaucracy*; and P. C. Lloyd, "African Kingdoms."

8. Nafa and Nafa's community are discussed more fully in chapter II.

9. CTBTH, Texts 901, 916, 926, and 954.

10. Evidence from the wider region of northern Busoga indicates that there were several Bakama in each northern kingdom during the last four decades or so of the nineteenth century. In Luuka, it appears that there was a Mukama in each of the major lineages of the ruling family in the 1880s. There is a hint in this of a purposive or necessary nature of Mukama possession in the society of the nineteenth century.

11. The most commonly recollected characteristic of the various recent Bakama is "light" skin. The heroic figure with "light" skin is a familiar theme in the twentieth-century litany of priests around the Lake Victoria region. In respect to Mukama of Bunafu, some texts recall this characteristic of "lightness," others "speaking in the womb," still others that "he was born with teeth." Of course, today, these are the characteristics that are supposed to identify Mukama possession, and sources may be imposing present-day ideas upon the fainter traditions of the nineteenth century. What is recalled, perhaps, is "what must have been" rather than "what was." What is clear is that the young Mukama had some characteristics that caused him to be perceived as possessed from his very first years.

12. CTBTH, Text 954.

13. For this region of Africa one can cite the observations of Burton, Baker, Speke, and Stanley.

14. There are various examples of both momentary and enduring religious complexes that were organized without reference to specific political boundaries. There are the cults associated with the *Cwezi* pantheons of the Lake Victoria region (Cohen, "Cwezi"). There are the *Wamara* and *Ryangombe* cults of Rwanda and the western grasslands (L. de Heusch, *Le Rwanda*). There is the *Nabingi* movement, which spread over a very wide region in the last decades of the nineteenth century (E. Hopkins, "Nyabingi"). In the twentieth century, there is the example of the *Maji Maji* movement which leaped rapidly past the boundaries of the extant political communities of central and southern Tanzania and created a new community of action. There are the Watchtower movements which spread across the colonial borders of central Africa. All bring into question the implicit model of the court as the generative center of action in Africa. The inquiries of nineteenth-century travelers, the determinism of colonial administration, and the selective political attentions of anthropologists and historians may have obscured the capacity of institutions beyond the courts to generate new ideas and forms, to become centers of change.

15. CTBTH, Text 954.

CHAPTER II: THE WORLD of NAFA

1. With the clear exception of the practice of planting trees to mark the boundaries of gardens and subvillages (*bisoko*).

2. This ideal is reflected in the behavior of the head of the compound and in the respect accorded the head by visitors. While a lineage may believe it has eternal rights to, and control over, a section of land (and its head behave as if this were so), in fact these "eternal" rights have quite frequently been violated by authorities and new settlers. Busoga "land law" is in fact today an extremely diffuse collection of conflicting ideals and considerations. The subject has been treated extensively by Lloyd A. Fallers, *Law Without Precedent*, pp. 200–255.

191

3. This picture of the difficult early years draws upon observations of new settlements along the sleeping-sickness frontier of southern Busoga.

4. There were numerous categories of specialists including, beyond those mentioned, drum makers, canoe builders, bonesetters, surgeons specializing in eye work, headaches, bites, and so forth, hunters, musicians, and ferrymen.

5. *Bafumu* (sing. *mufumu*) are doctors who treat illnesses or other problems directly through various means, including medication and spiritual healing. The *balaguzi* (sing. *mulaguzi*) are those specialists who preside over divination, the consultation of oracles, and communication with spirits of the dead.

6. The dispersals of Lungfish lineages are discussed in Cohen, *Historical Tradition*, pp. 93–100.

7. CTBTH, Texts 136, 137, 972, and 978.

8. The convulsions in southern Busoga, which may have given a push to these migrations from the Bunyuli area, are briefly mentioned in Cohen, *Historical Tradition*, pp. 120–123.

9. CTBTH, Texts 82, 963, and 1,010.

10. CTBTH, Texts 287, 288, and 1,005.

11. CTBTH, Texts 673–694, 1,008, and 1,009.

12. There has been no census of the population of Busoga in terms of clan affiliation. The 1969 Uganda Census recorded 896,875 persons in Busoga District. But one of the more than 240 clans in present-day Busoga, the Nangwe clan appears to number between 18,000 and 25,000. This estimate is based on a sampling of taxpayers recorded during the Village Survey.

13. On the *Bakenyi* (or *Bakenhe*), see Cohen, *Historical Tradition*, pp. 128–133 and pp. 179–180.

14. CTBTH, Texts 655–665, 910, 914, 975, and 997.

15. CTBTH, Texts 721–723. Y. K. Lubogo, *Busoga*, devotes nine pages to the history of the small Bukono state. While not explicitly mentioning the Baganza, he provides the names of seven "common people in Bukono who distinguished themselves for their bravery." Among the seven, three were Baganza. Of these, "Mutagaya" is probably the very same Mutagaya mentioned in the Muganza drumbeat slogan—"*Mutagaya adhooma, Buganza bututula*." ("Mutagaya comes stealthily, Buganza

beats.") One Mutagaya is considered to have been a leader of the Baganza who left Bukono and traveled westward (CTBTH, Texts 375–377).

16. CTBTH, Texts 371–379, 985, and 1,017.

17. John Lamphear, *Jie of Uganda*, pp. 125–126, 134–135, and 177–178.

18. Ibid., pp. 125–126.

19. "Kidolo was living when Womunafu first came to Bunafu. Womunafu came while he was hunting. He found Kidolo seated on his stool and asked him, 'If your fire is extinguished, where do you get a new flame?' Kidolo said that he would make a new fire himself and showed that Womunafu how to do it." (CTBTH, Text 1,017.) Kidolo was a Nafa. Interestingly, Lamphear, *Jie of Uganda*, p. 128, notes that one fire-making group in Jie established a prohibition against harming hyraxes or rock rabbits found at one very important place. The rock rabbit is the totem of the Muganza group in Busoga.

20. CTBTH, Texts 376, 378, and 379. A survey of *mutala* office holders in the late nineteenth century suggests that *mutala* Buhalira (in which the Kyanvuma shrine is located) long ago passed from the control of the Baganza to a lineage of the Nkwanga clan. (VS, "Buhalira," Vukula subcounty). It is clear that the Kyanvuma shrine at Buhalira, Bukono, was not a specific Muganza clan shrine, for it was visited by people of various other kin groups, including members of Mwebya and Nangwe lineages.

21. Fallers, *Bantu Bureaucracy*, pp. 102–125.

22. Ibid., pp. 113–114.

23. Ibid., p. 113.

24. Ibid., pp. 115–116.

25. Ibid., pp. 116–124.

CHAPTER III: THE YOUNG MUKAMA

1. See the discussion of chronology in the appendix.

2. J. Kasirye, *Abateregga*, pp. 35–38, A. Kaggwa, *Basekabaka*, pp. 76–86; and S. Kiwanuka, *Buganda*, pp. 136–137, are the principal sources on the reign of Kamanya.

3. Such a postulated drought is affirmed by a number of con-

temporary sources as well as by oral traditions collected in various parts of East Africa. See Cohen, "A Preliminary Study."

4. CTBTH, Texts 603, 613, 717, and 719; Lubogo, *Busoga*, p. 44.

5. VS, "Buyoga."

6. Patronage and clientship—and the relationship of these institutions to structures of authority and to patterns of social mobility—have received considerable attention from anthropologists and historians working in the Lake Victoria region. See L. Fallers, ed., *King's Men,* chapters 4–6; Fallers, *Bantu Bureaucracy*, chapters 6, 7, and 10; and M. Perlman, "Systems of Stratification," pp. 125–161.

7. CTBTH, Texts 915, 926, and 936.

8. These differences in the orientations and achievements of Lwo-speaking people in early northern Busoga are analyzed in Cohen, "Lwo Camps." Of the thirty Soga clans of apparent Lwo origin, only four or five were, in Busoga, royal clans—that is, providing the ruling dynasty of a state.

9. Records of clan affiliation of 572 partners in marriages in the neighborhood of nineteenth-century Bunafu constitute the sample upon which this observation is based. The data on clan affiliation are drawn from recorded genealogies. The Mukama is shown as a partner in twenty-one marriages in the sample.

10. This observation is based on the study of the maternity of twenty-one rulers of the three states. The evidence on the clan affiliation of mothers of princely children of lesser rank is poor, and an examination of these data would not permit one to extend the observation of the existence of a marriage prohibition to junior lineages of the royal houses. It is possible that the marriage restriction loosened beyond the senior lines.

Chapter IV: Bukanga

1. *Kanga* was the name of one, almost certainly the earliest, of Mukama's three spears. "Kanga" means "frighten" or "intimidate." *Kanga* is also recalled in the popular traditions of the heroic Mukama as a spear in the regalia of that figure, who is said to have crossed Busoga some generations earlier. The second

spear in the regalia of Mukama of Bunafu was known by the name *Kaweira ku luti*—"It is finished down to the very end," meaning, "The booty which was gotten from our last enemies is finished. We should return to battle and get more" (CTBTH, Text 936). The third spear was *Ntakaitawange*, meaning, "Since I have the power to kill my own people, what chance has my enemy" (CTBTH, Text 936). The names of the second and third spears suggest orientations with the later career of Mukama of Bunafu rather than the period in which the first enclosure was built. While no source explicit relates the etymology of the Bukanga enclosure name, the identification of the *Kanga* spear with that period seems reasonable, in that the important men and women at Makutu would have sought to emphasize symbols associated with the heroic Mukama—such as *Kanga*—and would have been at the center of the activities associated with the erection of the enclosure on the ridge.

2. This lacuna may actually be of advantage to the historian. Using evidence of a particularistic kind—evidence unselected by the organizing and reifying "logic" or "politic" of a popular conception of the past—the historian draws upon himself, and away from his sources, the task of reconstruction. The historian's edge here obviously lies in his being able to deploy a variety of methods, to use a wider range of evidence than that available to a particular community, and to maintain at least a marginal independence of legitimating considerations.

3. CTBTH, Texts 559–562, 935, and 937.

4. In the early part of the nineteenth century, the northward movement of the Luuka capitals appears to be part of a northward expansion of the state, coupled with an interest in maintaining the centrality of the court. In the later part of the century, this movement north appears to be a more "defensive" reaction to Ganda hegemony to the south and southwest of Luuka and to the extension of the *mbwa*-fly zone northward to the Kamirantumbu River. In the colonial period, the capitals again shift, this time to the south to bring the Luuka state closer to the headquarters of district administration. The shift north is also discussed in chapter VII.

5. The *ekyetoloolo* campaign of Sewankambo and his Ganda army is a marker in the traditions of many lineages throughout the

southern and eastern areas of Bugabula and the central areas of Luuka.

6. Kagoda granted control of five *mitala* to men of Nangwe lineages. CTBTH, Text 682.

7. There is essentially one popular etymology of the name "Womunafu," though the terms of explanation vary. There is a saying in Bunafu today, *"Ewomunafu negwa olugali."* (Literally, "It is at the lazy person's place that the winnow falls.") One source (CTBTH, Text 915) relates that "when a wife [of Womunafu] had many children, she would take some food from her gardens and keep it for her children. The first wife then would bring some of the remaining millet [to her husband] and put it in a tray and then the next wife would add her share, and the next, and then the next . . . whoever brought very little would be ridiculed, people saying, '*Ewomunafu negwa olugali.'* " ("At the lazy man's, the tray falls," or, "at Womunafu's ('the lazy one'), the tray falls because of overloading.") There is a second saying in Bunafu—*"Ewomunafu nebundwike."* A source (CTBTH, Text 926) relates, "It was in the thirty heaps of food brought by his women that he was called Womunafu. Every woman brought a heap of food and the later ones added their food to the first ones' pile. If one woman brought only a small amount to add . . . the others said, '*Ewomunafu nebundwike.'* ['It is at the lazy woman's that the winnow tipped.'] But his real name was Mukama." While neither explanation is overwhelmingly persuasive as an etymology, nor exhaustive of the possible sources of the name, the popular etymology does draw attention to an important pattern of service in precolonial Bunafu—the contribution of substantial quantities of food to the enclosure and the significant place of women as the source of this supply.

8. CTBTH, Text 1,018. The "Goat" is Wambuzi, the father of Womunafu and king of Luuka during the first half of the nineteenth century. "Wambuzi" means "Mr. Goat" and was the name accorded the king because he wore a small beard resembling that of a goat. "The Namunhole" refers to the mother of Mukama Womunafu who was of the Igobe clan and a girl whose antecedents came from Bunhole (Bunyuli) in southern Busoga. "Namutukula" is a nickname given to people with light or brown

196

skin. As "Mukama Namutukula" it has a double meaning, for it refers to both the lightness of Mukama Womunafu's skin (or to the "light spotches" on his forearms) and the Mukama or king of Bunyoro with the same nickname. He was Mukama Kyebambwe III, Namutukura, who is thought to have ruled Bunyoro in the late eighteenth and early nineteenth centuries.

CHAPTER V: KYONZIRA

1. CTBTH, Texts 463, 560, 745, and 914. The Soga traditions on the death of Kakuku do not mention the name of the Kabaka at the time of the execution. But it appears that Kakuku died in the last years of Kabaka Suna's reign. (Suna died ca. 1856.) Kaggwa, in *Kings* (Kiwanuka translation), pp. 131–132, relates two incidents in which important men from Busoga were executed in Buganda by order of King Suna. Both were associated with military campaigns organized in the last years before Suna's death. Kaggwa does not mention the fetid tribute at this point, but earlier in the narrative (p. 117), Kaggwa mentions an incident in which a large number of people were executed because of having left feces about. Kaggwa appears to locate this feces incident at a time in Suna's reign that falls before the death of Wambuzi and therefore before the accession of Kakuku. CTBTH, Text 914 relates that besides Kakuku, the highest-ranking chiefs of Luuka—Waidhuuba, Nagaya, Kakubampanga, and Makoma—were executed. Descendants of each of these men also relate that their antecedent was among those killed. CTBTH, Text 914 also relates that this last journey of Kakuku to Buganda was the fifth such trip. During these years, Soga chiefs made such journeys frequently, attempting to quiet Ganda military adventure in Busoga, making certain that neighboring chiefs were not setting them up for punishment. Text 914 relates that it was one of the rulers of Bulamogi whose man "untied the gifts and put feces in with them and then retied the parcels." The same source relates that the execution took place close to the Lake Victoria coast of Kyaggwe, near Nanso. CTBTH, Text 745 relates the manner of Kakuku's execution, "After they had set you on fire, they hung you. How could you escape death then?"

197

2. CTBTH, Text 134. STBTH, i, p. 71.

3. Cohen, *Historical Tradition*, pp. 174 and 177–178. CTBTH, Text 731.

4. See the discussion of Nafa as ritual specialist, chapter II.

5. See the discussion of Kabalu, chapter I.

6. See chapters VII and VIII for extended discussions of the roles of commoners in the accession of Mudhungu and in that of his son and successor Nabwana Inhensiko II.

7. CTBTH, Text 918. See further discussion of this shift north-ward, chapter VIII. The impact of the *mbwa* fly on another part of the Lake Victoria region is discussed in A. B. Raper and G. R. Ladkin, "Banakalanga," and in G. R. Barnley, "The Mbwa Fly." The Latin name of the fly is *Simulium damnosum Theo*. Scientific studies in this century have suggested that the fly (apart from giving a very nasty bite) may cause dwarfism in the population living within its range through affecting the functions of the pituitary and adrenal glands. Early European visitors to the region of eastern Buganda reported that the Banakalanga people of the Mabira (the great forest of Kyaggwe region) were genetically pygmoid. But Raper and Ladkin, among others, later demonstrated that not only was the dwarfism nongenetic, but also that the local population had for long recognized that the dwarfism was due to the fly-infested environment and that removal of an infant from the affected area would permit the child to develop normally.

8. CTBTH, Texts 955, 958, 965, 981, 996, and 998.

9. Fallers, *Bantu Bureaucracy*, chapters 6 and 7. See further remarks on this relational tension, chapter VII.

10. The seventh or eighth son of Mukama was Wambuzi Kabodi, named after Womunafu's father, King Wambuzi. The basis of the supposition that at least six sons had been born by Wambuzi's death is that Mukama Womunafu would have named a son "Wambuzi" immediately after, not before, Wambuzi's death.

CHAPTER VI: WOMUNAFU AND NAFA

1. See the discussion of "new supporters and old friends," chapter IV.

2. See the remarks on *buko*, chapter IV.

3. CTBTH, Texts 374–375, 377–378, 540, 542, 984, and 1,017.

4. CTBTH, Texts 540 and 542.

5. This observation of the openness of Bugabula is based upon an analysis of late nineteenth-century village (*mutala*) office holders and on the reconstruction of thousands of individual and family migrations in the Busoga region in the nineteenth century.

6. This trend was slowed—though certainly not halted—only in the 1870s after the seating of Mudhungu, the prince of the senior line and the favorite of the old commoners.

7. CTBTH, Text 1,017.

8. Earlier leaders of the Muganza lineage of Nafa Kyotaite of Bunafu are remembered as "Nafa," confounding this explanation of the name.

9. VS, "Bunafu." The descendants of Nafa living in Bunafu in 1971 were Kalisa Kyotaite, then about eighty years old but now deceased, his son Wilson Isabirye, born in 1938, and Wilson Isabirye's children. The data on Womunafu's lineage comes from a projection based on the Village Survey (VS). CTBTH, Text 926, provides an estimate of the numbers of taxpayers of Womunafu's lineage (89) which can be set against the number of taxpayers in Bunafu (approximately 200), giving a percentage of 44.5 of the population of Bunafu as members of Womunafu's patrilineage. Based on a total village population of approximately 1,000, this would have 445 descendants of Womunafu in the village. CTBTH, Text 927, the typescript of a notebook kept in the village which is reputed to contain the genealogies of members of Womunafu's lineage, but only in part, records about 230 living members of Womunafu's lineage. While the most specific source on the size of the lineage group, it certainly underrecords the descendants, particularly those under 10 years old, and it does not record the places of residence of the members of the lineage mentioned, possibly including therefore members of the lineage not living in Bunafu.

CHAPTER VII: REFLECTIONS OF A WIDER WORLD

1. S. Kiwanuka, *Buganda*, p. 167, "from about 1866 when

Mutesa was at the capital of Nakawa many Arabs came to the country, and with them came many trade goods. Cotton cloth spread extensively and the king allowed his subjects to wear kanzus and trousers. With this influence of Arabs and the desire to acquire more wealth, Mutesa lifted King Suna's ban on the selling of people. Thereupon chiefs sold into slavery men and women whom they obtained largely as a result of plunder." Mutesa may have maintained such an earlier ban on the external sale of slaves, but neither he nor his predecessor, Kabaka Suna, restricted the acquisition of slaves by Baganda in the early years. Kaggwa (*Basekabaka*) mentions some fourteen campaigns by Baganda to virtually every part of Busoga in the last years of Suna's reign (which ended ca. 1856) and through the first ten years of Mutesa's reign. Most of these campaigns were successful, and most brought back human plunder from Busoga. There are traditions from all over Busoga concerning the loss of men and women during this era of pillage and plunder. Some of these captives never reached Buganda, some were executed by the Baganda in Buganda or on the way back to Buganda, some survived the captive status and became functionaries or wives at the Ganda courts, and some, no telling how many, were sent down the long trade route to the Arab coast.

2. CTBTH, Texts 560, 561, 914, 917, and 935.

3. Martin Southwold, "Royal Succession," pp. 147–149, discusses the "structure" of a similar era of princes in Buganda: "in various ways fraternal succession made rebellions more likely. By preserving brothers as potential mature and strong successors, potential rebels were also preserved. Third brothers were apt to rebel lest they lose their chance of the throne; but this in turn provoked counter-rebellion from the filial generation. Younger full brothers were particularly dangerous, since their claim to the throne was exactly as good as that of their elders, and apparently for that reason their elders were unable to curb them. Finally, the fact of fraternal succession tended to inflate the number of princes—their sons and grandsons—eligible for the throne and therefore rivals for it."

4. CTBTH, Text 920.

5. The *ekitongole* was an administrative, service, or military

department directly under the Buganda king. The *ow'ekitongole* (or department head) was typically appointed by the king from among his royal pages or from among returning war heroes. The typical *kitongole* was formed to settle and defend newly incorporated regions along the Buganda frontier—to constitute a "barrack" of representation in areas not fully integrated into the kingdom. They were also used as organizing centers for campaigns outside the country and for provisioning the king and other officers of the state. By about 1860, Buganda controlled the southern or Bulondoganyi section of what is today Bugerere County. The area to the north was not incorporated until the last decade of the nineteenth century and then only with British assistance.

6. For Buganda and the Lake Victoria trade, see J. Tosh, "Interlacustrine Region," and G. Hartwig, "Victoria Nyanza."

7. CTBTH, Text 561.

8. CTBTH, Text 901.

9. The second-highest officer in the Buganda state was the *katikkiro*. In Busoga, there was an official called the *kitwikiro* who worked for a king or chief within his palace or enclosure as the person responsible for receiving visitors and for managing the day-to-day chores of the enclosure. In Buganda, the office of *katikkiro* had a large staff and enormous power; in Busoga, the staff was small, and the power did not radiate far. But toward the end of the nineteenth century, Soga rulers began to give additional responsibilities to these palace servants (or the servants themselves began to seize whatever opportunities arose). In Luuka, the *kitwikiro* began to carry the function of head of the army, and to the extent that the army was a standing one, this new function heightened the power of the once weak official. Tabingwa Nabwana Inhensiko's *kitwikiro* carried status and responsibilities not unlike that of the *katikkiro* of Buganda. It is likely that it was in this era that people in Busoga took as synonymous the two titles, whether or not the particular Soga official had in fact such great power.

10. CTBTH, Texts 914–915, 974, 997, and 1,018.

11. CTBTH, Texts 914 and 935.

12. Fallers, *Bantu Bureaucracy*, p. 231.

13. Nhiro, the first ruler of Luuka, had four sons. Inhensiko I,

the second ruler, had sixteen. Wambuzi had eight. Kakuku had two. Mudhungu had nine. Inhensiko II had five. The above numbers include only those men who survived to maturity, were granted estates, and left filial successors. They suggest the size of the royal family of Luuka just five or six generations after its beginning. A sample of the Luuka population undertaken in 1971–72 as part of the Village Survey indicates that between thirty and forty percent of the population of Luuka is of the royal patrilineage.

14. A. Southall, *Alur Society*, pp. 53–54, and "Rank and Stratification," p. 38; P. C. Lloyd, "African Kingdoms," pp. 95–96.

15. See the remarks on the size of Womunafu's lineage at the end of chapter VI and footnote 9 of that chapter.

16. See the section "Old Sons" in chapter V and map 16 in that chapter.

CHAPTER VIII: THE BWEBYA ILLNESS

1. Kaggwa, *Kings* (Kiwanuka translation), p. 173, mentions Balikumbuga as the Musoga appointed to lead this campaign to place Wambuzi on the throne of Luuka. Kaggwa relates that Balikumbuga had previously been appointed head of *Ekitongole Ekikubira*. CTBTH, Text 935 also mentions Bagoole Mwogezango, a man of the Kisige clan and brother of one of the divisional chiefs of Luuka, as being a leader of this campaign. Wambuzi Kyobe was the son of Kibalya of Naigobya and was attempting to succeed his father as ruler of Luuka. This claim naturally conflicted with that of Mudhungu who was the son of Kakuku, an elder brother of Kibalya. This episode is a good example of how disputes among brothers over succession can spill over into the next generation as long as the principle of legitimacy of fraternal succession endures. Mudhungu had advantages here, however, for he was the *eldest* son of Kakuku, who had been the *eldest* of his generation. As the eldest, Mudhungu was the only candidate available whose succession, and maintenance in office, could revivify the old principle of filial succession and thereby reduce the play of civil dispute arising out of the unraveling of the fraternal principle following the death of Kakuku. If Wambuzi Kyobe, with the help of his commoner allies, had managed to

succeed Kibalya, or to supplant Mudhungu, all the grandsons of
the late King Wambuzi would have had a strong basis for claim-
ing the stool of Luuka.

2. CTBTH, Texts 916 and 917.
3. CTBTH, Text 561.
4. Private communication, J. B. Webster.
5. VS, "Bulamogi."
6. VS, "Luuka."
7. CTBTH, Text 936.
8. CTBTH, Text 936.

CHAPTER IX: BUNAFU

1. CTBTH, Text 916.
2. *Karuoth* is the Lwo term for royal house. This opposition
between an individualized status and an exalted collateral group is
discussed at length in Cohen, "Lwo Camps."
3. Cohen, "Lwo Camps."

APPENDIX: THE CONSTRUCTION OF A CHRONOLOGY

1. H. M. Stanley, *Dark Continent*, i, pp. 362–363.
2. This genealogy is taken from S. Kiwanuka, *Buganda*, pp.
322ff.
3. The problems of using the "average generation" are discussed in Cohen, "Interlacustrine Chronology," pp. 193–197; D.
H. Jones, "African Chronology," pp. 166–168; and D. Henige,
"Oral Tradition and Chronology," pp. 371–389 and *Chronology
of Oral Tradition*, particularly chapter iv.
4. Kaggwa, *Kings* (Kiwanuka translation), p. 173. For discussion of *kitongole*, see note 5, chapter VII.
5. Ibid., p. 159.
6. Ibid., pp. 159–160.
7. Ibid., pp. 131–133. The quotation is from p. 132.
8. Richard Burton, *Lake Regions*, p. 403. The visitor was Snay
bin Amir.
9. J. H. Speke, *Journal of the Discovery*, pp. 280–415.
10. Stanley, *Dark Continent*, i, pp. 362–363.

11. Editorial notes attributed to J. M. Gray within "Chronology of Buganda 1800–1907, from Kaggwa's *Ebika*," translated by A. M. K. Mayanja, *Uganda Journal*, pp. 148–149; and J. M. Gray, "Ahmed Bin Ibrahim," p. 82. Burton, *Lake Regions*, p. 400, notes that Suna "reigned till 1857," his information apparently derived from later Arab travelers.

12. See "Kakuku's execution" above.

13. Kaggwa, *Kings* (Kiwanuka translation), pp. 103–112.

14. Ibid., p. 109.

15. See Cohen, "A Preliminary Study."

16. Kaggwa, *Kings* (Kiwanuka translation), p. 105.

17. Ibid., pp. 103–112.

18. R. Oliver, "Royal Tombs," pp. 124–133.

19. Cohen, "Interlacustrine Chronology," figures 4a and 4b, pp. 199ff.

20. Kaggwa, *Kings* (Kiwanuka translation), p. 47, notes an eclipse in the reign of Kabaka Juko: "Then the king wanted to have the man arrested. But the man threatened, 'If you want to arrest me, I shall order the sun to fall down.' Before Juuko [Juko] could reply, the doctor ordered the sun to set, and suddenly darkness enveloped the earth." The 1680 date is only one of several dates of eclipse visible in Buganda between the fifteenth and nineteenth centuries. Early eclipse maps indicated that the 1680 eclipse would have been total over central Buganda, but corrected maps indicate that it would have been partial, perhaps not significant at all. (R. Gray, "Eclipse Maps" and "Annular Eclipse Maps.") The postulation of the 1680 date for Juko's eclipse does not rest on the astronomical data but rather on the application of the twenty-seven-year average to the "average generation." D. Henige, "Reflections," p. 37, discounts the whole discussion of whether an eclipse is total or partial. His view is that it is not the astronomical phenomenon but the importance of the associated events that determines whether or not the eclipse will be long remembered. One might note that in the case of Juko's eclipse the associated events noted by Kaggwa were quite innocuous. By the same logic, might one postulate that if the associated events were of quite small importance and the eclipse remembered over a very long period, then the astronomical phenomenon must have been extraordinarily impressive?

Bibliography

Baker, S. W. *Albert N'yanza*. 2 vols. London; Macmillan and Co., 1866.

Barnley, G. R. "The Mbwa Fly and the Problems of its Control." *Uganda Journal* 16 (1952); 113–120.

Burton, Richard. *The Lake Regions of Central Africa*. 2 vols. London; Harper and Bros., 1860.

Cohen, D. W., ed. "Collected Texts: Busoga Traditional History," recorded in 1966-67 and 1971-72. Transcripts in possession of editor.

——. "The Cwezi Cult." *Journal of African History* 9 (1968); 651–657.

——. *The Historical Tradition of Busoga*. Oxford; Clarendon Press, 1972.

——. "Lwo Camps in Seventeenth Century Eastern Uganda." In *Proceedings of the Third International Congress of Africanists*, edited by B. A. Ogot. In press.

——. "A Preliminary Study of Climatic Trends in the Lakes Plateau Region of East Africa." Paper presented to the annual meeting of the African Studies Association, Chicago, 1974.

——. "The River-Lake Nilotes from the Fifteenth to the Nineteenth Century." In *Zamani: A Survey of East African History, New Edition*, edited by B. A. Ogot, pp. 135–149, Nairobi; East African Publishing House-Longman Kenya, 1974.

——, ed. *Selected Texts: Busoga Traditional History*. 3 vols. Xeroxed and bound edition deposited in CAMP Collection, Chicago, Illinois, and other Africana libraries.

——. "A Survey of Interlacustrine Chronology." *Journal of African History 11* (1970); 177–201.

——. "Village Survey, Busoga, Uganda." Survey of lower- and middle-level office holders and constituencies undertaken in 1971-72. Records in possession of author.

De Heusch, L. *Le Rwanda et la civilisation interlacustre*. Brussels; Université Libre de Bruxelles, 1966.

205

Bibliography

Fallers, L. A. *Bantu Bureaucracy*. Chicago and London; The University of Chicago Press, 1965.

————, ed. *The King's Men*. London; Oxford University Press, 1964.

————. *Law Without Precedent*. Chicago; The University of Chicago Press, 1969.

Gray, J. M. "Ahmed Bin Ibrahim—the First Arab to Reach Buganda." *Uganda Journal* 11 (1947); 80-97.

————, "Editorial Notes to 'Chronology to Buganda, 1800-1907, from Kaggwa's *Ebika*.'" *Uganda Journal* 16 (1952); 148–149.

Gray, Richard, "Annular Eclipse Maps." *Journal of African History* 9 (1968); 147–157.

————. "Eclipse Maps." *Journal of African History* 6 (1965); 251–262.

Hartwig, G. "The Victoria Nyanza as a Trade Route in the Nineteenth Century." *Journal of African History* 11 (1970); 535–552.

Henige, D. *The Chronology of Oral Tradition*. Oxford; Clarendon Press, 1974.

————. "Oral Tradition and Chronology." *Journal of African History* 12 (1971); 371–389.

————. "Reflections on Early Interlacustrine Chronology." *Journal of African History* 15 (1974); 27–46.

Hopkins, E. "The Nyabingi Cult of Southwestern Uganda," In *Rebellion in Black Africa*, edited by R. I. Rotberg, pp. 60–132. London; Oxford University Press, 1971.

Jones, D. H. "Problems of African Chronology." *Journal of African History* 11 (1970); 161–176.

Kaggwa, A. *Ekitabo kya Basekabaka be Buganda*. London; Macmillan and Co., 1901 and 1953.

————. *The Kings of Buganda*. Translated by M. S. Kiwanuka. Nairobi; East African Publishing House, 1971.

Kasirye, J. *Abateregga ku Namulondo ya Buganda*. London; East African Publishing House, 1959.

Kiwanuka, S. *A History of Buganda*. New York; Africana Publishing Corp., 1972.

Lamphear, J. *The Traditional History of the Jie of Uganda*. Oxford; Clarenden Press, 1976.

Bibliography

Lloyd, P. C. *"The Political Structure of African Kingdoms,"* In *Political Systems and the Distribution of Power,* edited by M. Banton, pp. 63–112. London; Tavistock Publications, 1968.

Lubogo, Y. K. *A History of Busoga.* Jinja, Uganda; East African Literature Bureau, 1962.

McMaster, D. N. *A Subsistence Crop Geography of Uganda.* Bude, Cornwall, England; Geographical Publications, 1962.

Oliver, R. "The Royal Tombs of Buganda." *Uganda Journal* 23 (1959); 124–133.

Perlman, M. "The Traditional Systems of Stratification Among the Ganda and the Nyoro of Uganda." In *Social Stratification in Africa*, edited by A. Tuden and L. Plotnikov, pp. 125–161. New York; The Free Press, 1970.

Raper, A. B., and Ladkin, G. R. "The Banakalanga of Kyagwe." *Uganda Journal* 15 (1951); 144–158.

Southall, A. *Alur Society.* Cambridge; W. Heffer and Sons, 1956.

———. "Rank and Stratification Among the Alur and Other Nilotic Peoples." In *Social Stratification in Africa,* edited by A. Tuden and L. Plotnikov, pp. 31–46. New York; The Free Press, 1970.

Southwold, M. "The History of a History: Royal Succession in Buganda." In *History and Social Anthropology*, edited by I. M. Lewis, pp. 127–151. London; Tavistock Publications, 1968.

Speke, J. H. *Journal of the Discovery of the Source of the Nile.* London; W. Blackwood and Sons, 1863.

Stanley, H. M. *Through the Dark Continent.* 2 vols. London; Harper and Brothers, 1878.

Tosh, J. "The Northern Interlacustrine Region." In *Pre-colonial African Trade*, edited by R. Gray and D. Birmingham, pp. 103–118. London; Oxford University Press, 1970.

Trevor-Roper, H. *The Rise of Christian Europe.* New York; Harcourt, Brace and World, 1965.

Vansina, J. "Once Upon a Time: Oral Tradition as History in Africa." *Daedalus* 100 (1971); 442–481.

———. *Oral Tradition.* Translated by H. M. Wright. London; Routledge and Kegan Paul, 1965.

Index

anthropology, 15; and history, 15-17

authority, 13, 29, 154, 156, 163ff; competition and conflict, 35-36, 69; deference to, 133; delegation to Bawalamayi, 141; discipline of princes, 128-30, 143-45, 155-56; eclipse of Nafa's, 127-28; enclosure design, 96-98; exercise by commoners, 139ff, 156; expansion of royal, 11, 163-65; formed and given, 158-59; Kadimo, 65; king's and Mukama's, 35, 37, 90, 164; Mukama as formula, 159, 163-65; Mukama's grants to sons, 119-21; Nafa's, 66; pressure of chief's kin, 117; range of Nyoro, 161-62; scope of Mukama Womunafu's, 154; sources of Mukama's, 82-83

bafumu, balaguzi, 50, 110; defined, 192

Baganza, 64, 111-13, 192-93. See also Muganza clan

baiwa (sing. mwiwa), 64-65; defined, 64

Bakama (sing. Mukama), 85, 190. See also Mukama

bako, see buko

balaguzi, 105. See also bafumu

balangira, see mulangira

baswezi (priests of spirit possession), 33, 34, 35-36, 37, 81

Bawalamayi of Mwebya clan,

140-42, 145, 146, 149, 173, 175

birth, of Mukama, 33-34, 36-37

bisoko, see kisoko

boundaries, 4, 39-40, 43; between Luuka and Bugabula, 95-96; natural, 39-40, 191; planted, 43

brideprice, as exchange mechanism, 51

Budiope, see Bugabula

Bugabula, 7, 8, 31, 44, 54, 57, 86, 100-101, 120-21, 134, 147-48, 173; ekyetoloolo campaign, 74, 76-77, 195-96; expansion of, 40, 76-77, 92-93, 103; mobility, 80; opportunities in, 128ff, 156; refugees from Bunafu, 128ff, 175-76, 178-79; and site of Bukanga enclosure, 91-92, 106

Buganda, 5, 8, 54, 58-59, 62, 67, 73, 75, 93, 106, 138-39, 146-47, 151, 156, 162, 170, 187-88; armies of, 73-74, 174-75, 179, 200-201; attack on Mudhungu, 146, 174-75; Bugabula's tribute, 78; demand for slaves, 51, 73, 82, 131-32, 200; demand for women, 132; dynastic genealogy, 171; ekyetoloolo campaign, 74ff, 90, 162, 180-82, 195-96; end of campaign, 78-79; "era of princes," 200; "feces" affair, 107, 176-77, 197; intrigue in Luuka, 133, 146; mobility, 80; settlement of

209

155-56, 189; under Nabwana Inhensiko II, 148-49

community, 69ff, 84, 121, 123, 155, 164; Bukanga as, 103ff; Bunafu and Luuka as,158; domination of, 133; end of Nafa's, 128; and chief's kin, 117-18; perception of larger world, 95-96, 131-32

conflict, and adventurers, 80-81; among Luuka, Bugabula, and Bulamogi, 92ff, 135ff; between: Buganda and Bunyoro, 73ff; idea of Mukama and kingship, 34-35; Mukama and Nafa, 69, 122, 123ff; young Mukama and Luuka court, 94. *See also* "era of princes"

drought, 77, 167, 180ff, 193-94

economy, 45ff, 134ff, 153; cultivation patterns, 41ff; markets and trade, 45, 47, 96, 134ff. *See also* land

ekyetoloolo campaign, 74ff, 98, 102, 116, 179, 180ff, 185, 195-96.

enclosure, 33, 40; changes in design, 149-51; isolation of, 33, 103ff; and Lwo speakers, 86-87; and Mukama, 34, 69, 72, 116, 121-22, 162-63; Nafa's last, 130; serial occupation of, 110ff, 170. *See also* Buganda, Bukanga, Bwebya, Twesudde

England, 151-52, 153, 201

"era of princes," 107-108, 115-16, 129-30, 132-33, 139, 157-58; in Buganda, 200; end of, 140. *See also* prince(s)

exchange, patterns of, 48ff. *See also* economy

Fallers, 69ff, 117, 143

famine, *see* drought

"following," 79ff; Mukama's 83ff; old and new support, 117-18

Ganda, *see* Buganda

Gray, J. M., 178

Henige, D., 204

history, 14; and anthropology, 15-16; and past, 14

ideology, 158

Igobe, *see* clans

Inhensiko I, second ruler of Luuka, 23, 24, 25, 27, 28, 30, 31, 54, 56, 69, 85, 170, 182-83, 185, 189, 201-202; alliance with commoners, 28-29, 139; flight of families from, 52ff, 57

Inhensiko II, *see* Nabwana Inhensiko II

iron production and trade, 45, 47, 49, 134-35

Junju, Kabaka of Buganda, 58-59, 75-76, 171

Kabalu, mother of Wambuzi Munhana, 23, 25, 90, 107, 116, 138, 177, 189; ideological struggle, 158; Wambuzi Munhana, 24-25

Kaggwa, A., 174, 177, 180-81, 182, 197, 202, 204

Kagoda, ruler of Bugabula, 74, 76ff, 92ff, 100, 162, 175-76,

Wagubona, husband of Lubagu, 3, 5ff, 58, 128, 173, 178, 182ff

Wambuzi Munhana, ruler of Luuka, 24, 25, 28, 30ff, 57, 69, 97, 106, 107, 116, 119, 133, 162, 170, 173, 179-80, 182-83, 185, 189, 190, 196, 197, 202-203; attacked by Buganda, 74, 78, 82; birth of son Mukama Womunafu, 34, 37-38; and commoners, 28-29; and Kagoda of Bugabula, 93; and Mukanni, 26, 30, 37, 52; and site of Bukanga enclosure, 89ff, 94, 98; succession of 25, 26, 80

Womunafu, *see* Mukama

LIBRARY OF CONGRESS CATALOGING IN PUBLICATION DATA

Cohen, David William.
   Womunafu's Bunafu: a study of authority in a
nineteenth-century African community.

   Bibliography: p.
   Includes index.
   1. Womunafu, Mukama, 1830?-1906.   2. Soga (Bantu
tribe)—Politics and government.   3. Soga (Bantu tribe)
—Kings and rulers—(Biography).   I. Title.
DT433.242.W65C64   967.6'101'0924 [B]   77-71976
ISBN 0-691-03093-6